Verena Anker

Digital Dance

Verena Anker

Digital Dance

The Effects of Interaction between New
Technologies and Dance Performance

VDM Verlag Dr. Müller

Imprint

Bibliographic information by the German National Library: The German National Library lists this publication at the German National Bibliography; detailed bibliographic information is available on the Internet at http://dnb.d-nb.de.

Cover image: www.purestockx.com

Publisher:
VDM Verlag Dr. Müller Aktiengesellschaft & Co. KG, Dudweiler Landstr. 125 a, 66123 Saarbrücken, Germany,
Phone +49 681 9100-698, Fax +49 681 9100-988,
Email: info@vdm-verlag.de

Produced in USA and UK by:
Lightning Source Inc., La Vergne, Tennessee, USA
Lightning Source UK Ltd., Milton Keynes, UK
BookSurge LLC, 5341 Dorchester Road, Suite 16, North Charleston, SC 29418, USA

ISBN: 978-3-639-00364-2

Contents

Illustrations

Figure 1.1   Dance Works, Studio chart showing floor directions, 1998. Retrieved March 20, 2006 from http://www.danceworksonline.co.uk/syllabus/terminology_ballet_grades.htm, page 12

Figure 2.1   Richard James Lane, Marie Taglioni, ca. 1825-1850. Retrieved March 20, 2006, from http://ballettgeschichte.de/bildergalerie/24a6bc95a8117a00d/1004.jpg, page 20

Figure 2.2   Sakhraprom, pointe shoes, 2005. Retrieved March 21st, 2006, from http://bmw.sakhaprom.ru/p/52/images/pro-quiet-2007-pointe-shoe-p2007.jpg, page 22

Figure 2.3   Bloch, thong, naked dancer's feet, 2004. Retrieved March 21st, 2006, from http://www.dancesuppliesusa.com/lyrical_shoes.html, page 22

Figure 2.4   Didier Mulleras, mini@tures 5, photography of video performance, 2004. Retrieved April 2nd, 2006, from http://www.mulleras.com, page 25

Figure 2.5   Didier Mulleras, mini@tures 8, photography of video performance, 2004. Retrieved April 2nd, 2006, from http://www.mulleras.com, page 25

Figure 2.6   Bobby Bodenheimer, Typical Motion Capture Setup, 2000. Retrieved May 16, 2006, from http://www.vuse.vanderbilt.edu/~bobbyb/images/Linda.html, page 29

Figure 2.7   Chris Bregler, optical motion capture suit, 2003. Retrieved May 16, 2006, from http://movement.nyu.edu/projects/lma/pictures.html, page 34

Figure 2.8   Paul Kaiser & Shelley Eshkar, BIPED Merce Cunningham Dance Company Projections, virtual figure animated through Motion Capturing, 1999. Retrieved May 20, 2006, from http://www.ispa.org/features/ny2001.html, page 36

Figure 3.1   Garry Mason, screenshot of wire-framed model in *Poser* menu, 2003. Retrieved   June 20, 2006, from http://www.gkmason.com/tutorials/sten3.htm, page 48

Figure 3.2   Garry Mason, screenshot of naked model in *Poser* menu, 2003. Retrieved June 20, 2006, from http://www.gkmason.com/tutorials/stencils.htm, page 48

Figure 3.3   Garry Mason, screenshot of clad model in *Poser* menu, 2003. Retrieved June 20, 2006, from http://www.gkmason.com/tutorials/stencils.htm, page 48

Introduction

> On the sombre stage, only the dancer's half-naked body is spotlighted. His
> slow and trance-like movements make appear every working muscle of his
> body which is exclusively clad in wide cotton trousers. Suddenly, the man
> stops moving: a second dancer enters the stage. More precisely, he enters
> the stage in flying, his arms widespread. If he appears to be spatially close
> to the audience at one moment, he seems to be at large distance in the next
> second. When the two dancers start to perform a pas de deux[1], the second
> body appears weightless compared to his partner. Moreover, he does not
> wear any cloth at all. 'He' is a three-dimensional virtual projection.

Although the previously described scenery refers to an existing choreography[1], it still might possess a fictional character for certain readers. This impression is certainly due to the idea of dance combined with digital images, thus with computer technologies. Because "dance, the art of human movement, is something expressed with the physical body, and on the surface appears nontechnologically inclined" (Gray, 1989:1; Kepner, 1997:12), and consequently "any technological aid or intervention [would be] seen as an inappropriate substitute for the true nature of the art form" (Kepner, 1997:12). This aspect seems especially valid in the case of New Technologies[2], as the abstract and immaterial character of digitalisation, i.e. the decomposition of objects into pixels, appears contradictory to the flesh and bones serving as material for dance performance. Here, algorithmic calculation and thus a high degree of formalism seem incompatible with the human and physical art of dance.

How can dance performance survive in the post-modern era, in "a time when the individual [is] in danger of being disembodied, sucked into cyberspace or modified by the tools of biotechnology" (Berghaus, 2005:75)? Is the integration of New Media into dance art likely to suffocate the dancer's body in a post-organic spectacle? Questions of this kind might come up when reflecting on 'multimedia performance', that is dance productions including New Technologies. However, in this context it is worth mentioning that different technological

---

[1] The described tableau is part of *Double Cue*, a work of the French dancer and choreographer Patrice Barthès. This choreography will be analysed as a case study in ch. 3.
[2] The term 'New Technologies', commonly also known as New Media, refers to electronical devices and applications based on digital computerised processes. New Media are considered as new communication forms as they connect different
elements such as image, text and tone, which were only separately present in the so-called old media such as books, radio, and television (Manovich, 2001).

devices such as the pointe shoe, theatrical lighting or video cameras have been used to produce or enhance various effects during the performance of dances for decades[3]; technology thus has constantly accompanied and influenced the evolution of dance art. This fact evidently implies that also the dancer's body has been confronted with diverse technologies. At first sight, the combination of man and (technological) instrument appears contradictory, as "to dance is human [and] to operate machines is inhuman" (Gray, 1989:123), but a closer look at dance reveals that this performing art form relies on a clearly defined and applied technique which renders the body itself into a highly learned instrument. Thus dance, and with it the human body, are not confronted with technology in complete dichotomy but are rather related to it. This means that during the development of dance, performers have engaged their bodies into relations with diverse technological devices in order to integrate them into their performances. To what extent can the human body itself be considered as a technology? And what exactly happens to the 'body-instrument' when meeting (new) technologies? How does the choreo-technical relation between body and machine affect the concrete dance performance?

The aim of this thesis being an analysis of technologies' effects on dance performance, its focus will be centred on the use of New Media in artistic dance productions. In presenting the ways in which dancers engage with (new) technologies, I want to observe whether and how their bodies overcome the sharp boundary between organic materiality and the "cold and disembodying effect" (Portanova, 2005) of (computer) technology.

An important part of my research is based on specialised literature concerning dance and New Technologies. The number of works dealing with the concrete connection of dance and digital media still being rather limited, I also consulted studies of the performing arts in general. Moreover, my theoretical research is completed by the knowledge I gained through diverse interviews held with artists and choreographers who currently integrate multimedia technology into their creations. The observations made during my field studies related to the work of the French choreographer Patrice Barthès added precious value to my findings.

The first chapter will allow me to present a brief outline about dance characteristics and show to what extent this physical art adopts formal and 'technological' features and in which way the human body itself can be understood as man's "ultimate technology" (De Spain, 2000:2). The second chapter will then deal with the ways different 'old' and new technologies were and are introduced to dance; here, a clear focus will be put on their effect on the dancing body. In the third chapter, I will present Barthès' creation *Double Cue* in order to analyse the consequences of

---

[3] Evert (2003).

computer technology's concrete integration into a choreographic artwork. In this context, my study will not limit itself on the piece's description but it will also provide an insight into *Double Cue*'s creative process, allowing me to figure out how the dancer's body enters into contact with a digitally created character and therewith to detect "the potentials [human and New Technologies] can bring to light by coming together" (Portanova, 2005). This argumentation leads to the conclusion which will answer the problem statement of this thesis: How do New Technologies affect performance in contemporary dance productions?

1. Dance rationalising the concept of the human body

1.1 A definition of dance as an art form

Dance is the art of moving the human body according to a structure in space and time[4].

De Leeuwe & Uitman (1966:17)

In an interview with John Cranko[5], Erich Walter[6] formulated the following phrase: "I want to ask a question which we cannot answer. ... The one asking why, in certain situations, human beings stop speaking and start singing and dancing" (Cranko, 1974:26). This question refers to dance as an expression of emotions, mostly engendered spontaneously and therefore appearing as an inherent, if not primal instinct. Or, as Alexander Bland puts it: "Rhythmic movement is a concomitant of life ... and a natural reaction to emotion, from the ape rocking on his shelf to a human head rolling in extremities of grief or sexual bliss" (Bland, 1976:10). Thus, the idea of naturalness and irrationality are well reflected in this concept of dance understood as being part of human behaviour.

Nevertheless, since the very beginnings of mankind, the rhythmic movement of human beings has also been ritualised and accompanied different ceremonies in various cultures[7]. It is in this context that dance has developed into a highly stylised discipline in modern societies, reflecting cultural conditions, norms and values: it is the question of dance as a theatrical art form.

What exactly makes dance an art? Certainly, it is not only the sheer beauty of physical movement, its aesthetics, which give dance its artistic status[8]. Overall, the creation of a dance piece has to be considered in order to situate the context in which the concrete dance movement is performed. True to the idea that every artwork has a message to transmit, the choreographer Jacqueline Smith-Autard understands dance as an art if it has the intention to communicate a topic, that means its intention to transmit a story, emotions, or simply to tell movement itself[9]. Another important feature constituting artistic dance, still according to Smith-Autard, is "the expression or embodiment of something formed from diverse but compatible elements as a *whole*

---

[4] "De dans is de kunst het menselijk lichaam te bewegen volgens ordening in ruimte en tijd."
[5] John Cranko has been the artistic directore of the German Ballett Stuttgart from 1960 to 1973.
[6] Erich Walter has been the general manager of the German Baden-Württemberg Theater from 1949 to 1972.
[7] Bland (1976).
[8] In this context, the choreographer Jacqueline Smith-Autard explains that the "beauty of physical movement is aesthetically appreciated in many fields – athletics, sport, gymnastics, swimming, but this is not art" (Smith-Autard, 2004:5)
[9] Smith-Autard (2004).

entity to be enjoyed aesthetically .... To transform a vocabulary of movement into meaningful visual images, the composer is dealing with three intangible elements: movement, time and space" (Smith-Autard, 2004:5,17). Thus, within the idea of expressing the creator's intentions, the basic elements of dance have to be combined, or, in artistic language, composed.

This means that not only the human body's various expressive movements are structured in an intended way, for example defined by a certain style, but also its performance in space is given. As movement can be understood as an act of displacement, it is clear that a certain space is used, whether on a defined place on the ground or in the air. But also an immobile body occupies a certain space by its simple presence, and this space has to be defined, too.

Dance also exists through time because every movement demands a certain duration, or length[10]. In the performing arts, this characteristic too is used in a constructive way. For example, the combination of movements with varying durations allows the creation of rhythms and time patterns expressing the composition's main idea. In this context, dance can be understood as an effective combination dealing with the three elements of movement, time and space in order to express its creator's intention. The composition's unity is supposed to form specific images which themselves are supposed to provoke certain associations in the heads of its spectators.

Thus the choreography, i.e. the composition of a dance artwork, reveals itself as a highly complex task, demanding the structuring and coordination of different parameters. It goes without saying that for the creation of a dance piece, a high degree of creativity is necessary; nevertheless, it is also subject to a certain degree of rational thinking.

While this aspect is relevant for the choreographer's work, it is also of utmost importance for the performer, thus the dancer, as his body's movement provides one of dance's basic elements. As already explained, the presence of a (pre-)defined structure in dance art shows that to a certain degree, the dancer's movement is rationalised as it is formalised in numerous aspects. Therefore, it is necessary to analyse what dance's formalisation means for its performer. In a choreography but also in usual training sessions, the dancer orients his movements with respect to room directions which are clearly defined by numbers or special abbreviations (fig. 1.1); his body's performed positions are geometrically described and even

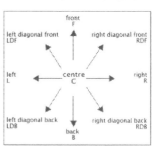

Figure 1.1: this chart presents the abbreviations used for the different room directions in dance

---

[10] ibid.

numerically fixed. For example, a dancer puts his feet into position number one, two, or three, turns himself around 180 degrees, or lifts his leg up to 90 degrees in order to perform an *écarté*, which is a classic dance position[11]. Also time is measured, mostly in succeeding sequences of eight beats. Thus, the movement is not only fixed in style and space, but also in time. In this perspective, each element constituting dance art is calculated and clearly defined. Here, we see that the body is taken out of a certain context and staged for the audience's perception; it has to obey the rules imposed by the choreography and its aesthetics in order to achieve its effect. For this, overcoming physical limits through extensive training is necessary. The dancer has to master a specific dance technique, that is the different parameters of a certain style to perfection, as it is only then that the highly stylised and precisely defined movements are presented as if no physical effort is needed for their performance.

However, the context of formalisation does not reduce itself to the presentation of choreographies, as also the usual training lessons and rehearsals resemble a schematised work process rather than the expression of pure emotion. During the past centuries, dance training has developed in order to bring the performer's body to its highest performance in terms of mobility, dynamic and control. Thus, the dancing body is formed in order to fit into the demands of its art. This does not only mean that the audience of a performance watches the result of disciplined and hard years of learning and training; the dancer's physical conscience has also been affected by rationalism. His knowledge about the body refers to anatomic and medical reasoning, allowing him to know how to use his body in order to achieve its maximal performance. He is for example aware of the fact that a well-balanced basin makes a higher leg lift possible, or which exercises optimise his muscular system's flexibility[12].

Also the newest achievements of modern comforts are applied to dance for improving performance conditions and perfect the final result, such as Sarah Schlesinger states: "In the beginning of the 21st century [dancers] find that the surfaces [they] dance upon have changed from traditional hardwood floors to Marley-type surfaces[13]. Even the air dancers breathe is different. Open windows in studios ... have been closed to accommodate air conditioning or other ways to artificially circulate air" (Barringer & Schlesinger, 2004:viii).

---

[11] In this position, the dancer's body is kept up straight while his leg, turned in outward position, is lifted up to a distance of 90 degrees from his supporting leg.
[12] In this context, it is interesting to note that numerous manuals for professional dance training present a big resemblance to works treating medical anatomy. See for example Franklin, Eric (2004). *Conditioning for Dance*. Leeds: Human Kinetics.
[13] Marley dance floors are vinyl floors made of very durable, heavy duty and slip resistant material. For more information visit http://www.danceequipmentintl.com/content/mfloors.html (retrieved April 10, 2006).

Constantly integrating itself into logical thinking patterns, optimising the training process and having established a proper technique concerning human movement, dance draws visible parallels to scientific thinking. This idea is also reflected by the fact that Western dance education is based on a classic style, which is also referred to as 'academic'. In this context, it is worth mentioning that also dance schools are commonly entitled as 'dance academies'[14]. Here, dance reveals as a very formal and structured process and thus appears completely separated from Bland's previously mentioned idea of dance as a natural reaction to emotion.

1.2 The dancing body mechanised

The context of human movement's formalisation in artistic dance has an important influence on the concept of the body. Each dancing style has its proper repertoire of steps and movements and thus possesses a specialised knowledge of 'handling' the body, of knowing how to use it in order to perform the demanded exercise. As already mentioned, this knowledge and skill are also referred to as 'dance technique'. Although the ability of expression and presentation is an important part of dance performance, it is a dancer's technical capacities allowing him the status of an artist, as his skill concerning the movements' performance cannot be achieved by untrained persons[15]. The application of movement patterns has consequences on the dancer's physical shape, as the latter is formed by intensive training. Thus, professional dancers' bodies distinguish themselves mostly through their extreme flexibility, the outward position of shoulders and legs, and extremely convoluted footbones among female dancers who are practicing the pointe technique[16].

Evidently, the dancing body becomes subject to and is affected by outer technical paradigms; it becomes a highly learned corpus as during the process of education, the dancer learns to know and master every part of his body and push it against its anatomical limits. In this context, the body becomes an instrument[17]; the dancer uses his body as a means in order to perform his art, as the dancing body's final aim is to be staged and become subject to the artistic *mise en scène*.

---

[14] The term dance academy is due to the growing importance of technical skills during the 17th century. The first 'Académie Royale de Danse', founded in 1661 in Paris by Louis XIV, established numerous rules concerned dance movements (De Leeuwe & Uitman, 1966).

[15] Smith-Autard (2004).

[16] The pointe technique refers to the movement on toes, which is executed with the help of the pointe shoe. See also ch. 2.1.

[17] This metaphor is also used by John Cranko stating that "the work with dancers resembles the tuning of a piano or a violin", adding that "a body must have a certain education …. One has to start quite young" (Cranko, 1974:57).

It is also in this context that the idea of the dancing body's mechanisation and its relation to technology becomes obvious, as the idea of the performing body as an instrument gives it a technical character. In order to integrate and perform artificial movements which, originally, were not part of it, the body applies a certain craft and knowledge. Moreover, its movement repertoire is acquired through continual work, which especially implicates the aspect of repetition: in order to perform the required non-inherent movements correctly, the dancer has to repeat them until his body 'functions'. This means that repetition is effectuated until the moment the dancer does not move with an important amount of consciousness and effort but rather activates a certain mechanism. In this moment, the dance technique is 'embodied', it has entered into the dancer's movement repertoire. This process can be designed as mechanisation, as this term refers to the action of "producing by or as if by [a] machine"[18]. In the same time, this idea draws a parallel to technology, which signifies the "systematic treatment of an art or craft"[19]. Also technique and technology are similar as both terms stand for the application of knowledge for a practical aim[20]. Nevertheless, from an anthropological point of view, the idea of technology extends itself to a social meaning, as it refers to the application of a knowledge which is influenced by social norms and conditions[21]. Also in dance, technique is applied to achieve a concrete result, that is the moment of performance. Moreover, this performance, and especially its aesthetics reflect the norms, thoughts and tastes of the society it is created in, as I will explain in the following chapters. Within this reasoning, it becomes clear that "dance and technique [as well as technology] – as knowledge about methods and practices for the generation of specific movements – are intrinsically tied to each other"[22] (Evert, 2003:7).

1.3 Body Technologies

The attribution of formal and mechanical qualities to the human body might appear as unnatural and even provoke the idea of a body-machine. Nowadays explicated by the concept of the

---

[18] The present definition can be found in the online-version of the encycolpaedia britannica (retrieved April 2nd, 2006, from www.britannica.com).
[19] ibid.
[20] In the online-version of Webster's Dictionary, both technique and technology are defined through "the application of knowledge (in view of) some 'practical' result" (retrieved March 30, 2006, from www.answers.com).
[21] The online-version of Webster's Dictionary defines technology in an anthropological sense as "the body of knowledge available to a society that is of use in ... practicing manual arts and skills" (retrieved March 30, 2006, from www.answers.com).
[22] "Tanz und Technik – als Wissen über Methoden und Verfahren der Erzeugung von spezifischen Bewegungen – sind untrennbar miteinander verbunden"

cyborg[23], this thought is also present in common comparisons with the heart or the brain as the human motor, for example. Here, the body is considered and understood as a mechanism designed for the achievement of specific aims.

If this aspect is true in a general sense, it is especially valid in the context of dance. As here, the human body is able to move and experience time and space in an acquired manner, no technological artefact nor technical device created this capacity; the body provoked its proper mechanisation. Therefore, it can be considered as a technology itself. This idea joins Marcel Mauss' anthropologist concept of the techniques of the body, stating that "before instrumental techniques there is the ensemble of techniques of the body. ... Man's first and most natural technical object, and at the same time technical means, is his body" (Mauss, 1992:461). In his article 'Techniques of the Body', Mauss not only acknowledges a social source to technology; he also mentions its traditional quality in referring to the (oral) transmission of knowledge in human cultures[24]. It is the learning from mimetic imitation which corresponds to this traditional character in dance.

Following this perspective, the human body can never be considered as 'natural' and free from exterior influences because each knowledge and behaviour is transmitted and thus evidently acquired in a social and cultural context. Thus, the body can be understood as a carrier of exterior influences which is always moulded and learned to a certain degree. Here it becomes obvious that dance never represents but "a natural reaction to emotion" as explained by Bland (1976:10), as each performed gesture is the result of previous appropriation. Thus, the difference between the spontaneous movement of a human and dance as an art form lies in the degree of the body's instruction: while impulsive movement has been learned on a rather unconscious level, academic dance refers to the conscious adoption of clearly defined exercises. As the preceding section has shown, through its highly developed technique, artistic dance appears as an excelling form of human movement which forms the professional dancer's body into an extremely learned instrument.

Still according to Mauss, not only the body represents a potential technology, as also diverse (technical) artefacts, thus products of technological processes, can be considered as such. Exterior to the human body, man applies them in order to widen his possibilities of moving but also of learning. In this context, Mike Michael introduces the distinction between 'epochal' and 'mundane' technologies. While the adjective 'epochal' designs the technologies having appeared

---

[23] This term refers to a living organism composed by a combination of human and machinal parts.
[24] Mauss (1992).

in a specific period and drastically created cultural changes, such as technologies of representation and transport like photography and automobile technology, Michael qualifies mundane technologies as "invisible" (Michael, 2000:108), as they represent mere objects which have shaped the human body's practices and functioning[25], such as walking shoes and sticks.

Thus, we can understand technology as that which enables the human body to achieve specific (practical) aims, whether it is a certain artefact, such as walking sticks, or a learned action accomplished through the body itself. In this sense, technology is represented by an external means, as originally it is not inherent, enabling the human being to exert that which he otherwise would be incapable of: in short, it can be understood as a broadening of man's possibilities, as an extension of his performance. Hence, applied to the context of dance, Mauss' concept clarifies that not only the dancer's body itself represents an instrument, but also technologies exterior to the human corpus have the potential to be used as instruments for the body.

The idea of the human body being constantly formed according to social and technological conditions[26] finds itself reflected in and through dance. In the following chapter, I will describe how examples of both mundane and epochal technologies have accompanied and influenced the evolution of dance performance in order to investigate the effect of digital technologies' advent on stage afterwards.

---

[25] Michael (2000).
[26] Mauss (1992).

2. Dance and (New) Technologies

When talking about the relation between theatre and technology, mostly the design of what I am calling ... 'the spatial surrounding of the actors' is mentioned. However, theatre technology does not leave the actors' performances unaffected. The 'contact' can be modest ... but also very intervening[27]

If Jacques de Vroomen's statement is referring to theatre performance, it is equally pertinent in the context of theatrical dance art. It is true that since its very beginnings, dance has always integrated technologies in order to enhance various aspects of the presented pieces. Nevertheless, in many cases the relation between technology and dance is limited to certain stage effects, or to that which De Vroomen describes as "the spatial surrounding of the performers" (2001). But we can also observe that technology has, and still does influence the performance itself, or as the researcher Judith A. Gray formulates: "Technology has historically affected the dance art product and the art-making process" (Gray, 1989:5). Consequently, technology engrains itself in dance technique and aesthetics as well as in the performing body.

While this effect is true for the concrete use of technology on stage, its influence is already present on a more general level: representing part of a society's cultural good, dance also reflects the social context it is created in[28]. In this perspective, technology already influences dance as it has an effect on the social attitudes and circumstances in which choreographic artworks are created and perceived. For instance, as this text will show, the main characteristics of Romantic Ballet correspond to the Zeitgeist of its epoch, stamped by the spirit of the Industrial Revolution.

This aspect being situated in a broader context, I will now consider the integration of different technologies which have influenced dance performance as well as its creation at distinct epochs. This will allow me to study the influence of digital technologies on stage afterwards. The example of the pointe shoe will demonstrate in how far a mundane technology engrains itself into dance performance as well as its aesthetics. While here, especially the human body's movements are affected, it is equally the notions of time and space on stage which will be influenced by the epochal technology of video. Which kind of relation does emerge between these two

---

[27] "Als we het hebben over de relatie van theater en techniek, gaat het vaak over de vormgeving van wat ik hierboven 'de ruimtelijke omgeving van de spelers' noemde. Theatertechniek laat het spel van de spelers echter niet onberoerd. De 'beroering' kan bescheiden, een enkel spotje, maar ook zeer ingrijpend zijn."
[28] Evert (2003).

technologies and the performing body? And does this relation alter when it comes to 'multimedia performance'?

2.1 The contribution of the pointe shoe in the epoch of Romantic ballet

In the history of theatrical dance, the pointe shoe can certainly be considered as a mundane technology which had a strong and direct impact on dance performance and therewith on its aesthetics.

The pointe shoe's invention in the beginning of the 19th century is rooted in the social context of the Industrial Revolution, an epoch witnessing the increasing use of machines as well as the resulting mechanisation of people's lives in Western societies. The overall industrial progress due to the use of machines granted a growing importance to diverse technologies and effectively demonstrated their superior power to human capacities. It is precisely in this context that the idea of scientism, the trust in scientific progress as an explanation of and a solution for diverse mundane problems[29], emerged. The use of machines as well as the application of rational, scientific knowledge enabled human beings to understand and even master phenomena which had been hitherto unexplainable. Nowadays, scientism seems to be reigning the modern world: the control of human and natural processes hits its peak in gene technology, permitting the artificial production of human beings. However, it is in the end of the 18th century that the Romantic movement, lauding the ideal of transcending humanity and making reappear mythical creatures such as elves and fairies, came up.

With its philosophy of overcoming anatomical boundaries, dance revealed as an appropriate cultural manifestation at this epoch, or as Ivor Guest puts it, "ballet was specially suited to express the ideas of the Romantic movement" (Guest, 1972:10). The ideal of exceeding human nature was even reinforced through the figure of the Romantic ballerina and her rather ethereal than human appearance; according to Kerstin Evert, "the ballerina and the ephemeral female fairy creature ... are not subject to gravity and thus epitomise the dream of the human body's transcendence" [30] (Evert, 2003:112). In order to highlight her weightlessness which was already suggested by light and fluid movements, the flying machine, already used in theatre from the 17th century onwards, allowed the ballerina to fly across the stage with the help of hidden wires. The

---

[29] retrieved June 12, 2006, from http://www.britannica.com

[30] "Die Ballerina bzw. das ... ephemere weibliche Feenwesen unterliegt nicht den Bedingungen der Schwerkraft und versinnbildlicht damit den Traum von der Transzendierung des menschlichen Körpers"

use of recently developed gas lights provided the tableau with a gloomy atmosphere and shimmering effects and thus made the illusion appear even more realistic. Here, we already see that different mundane technologies were used in order to enhance the performance's impact. Nevertheless, neither the gas lights nor the flying machine had a direct influence on the dancer's body and its movements as they did not affect the body's performance *per se*.

It is the use of the pointe shoe which rendered the illusion of the floating dancer even more

realistic, as its texture allowed the (female) dancer to move and balance on her fully stretched toes. With the help of the pointe technique, the ballerina culminated her image of an ethereal, supernatural being, and it is notable that the first choreography integrating a full part of pointe dance was significantly entitled *The Sylph*[31] (fig. 2.1). Nevertheless, the pointe shoe not only helped epitomise the major theme of Romantic ballet and Romanticism in general, it also affected dance performance in a substantial manner.

As the figure of the 'floating' dancer was highly acclaimed by its romantic audience, a growing number of artists added the technology of the pointe shoe to their repertoires. In the beginning, a dancer would rise to the tips of her toes only once during the entire performance,

Figure 2.1: the ideal of the romantic ballerina, represented by Marie Taglioni in 'The Sylph' (1832)

standing still in order to underline the pointe shoe's miraculous effect[32]. Those moments resemble an explicit presentation of the dance shoe and thus demonstrate that this technology was not yet considered as an integral part of the artist's performance, or as Barringer & Schlesinger put it: "These earliest appearances on pointe ... represented isolated *tours de force*[33], and were not yet part of the fabric of dance technique" (2004:3). Nevertheless, the dancing shoe's effect did not leave the audience indifferent as pointe performance was "enthusiastically received" in the theatres (2004:1). Consequently, the use of pointe shoes, and with it the artistic level of pointe dance, increased as a growing number of technical difficulties were demonstrated. This means that movements which were specially suited to the new technology were introduced and thus influenced the style and technique of dance at that time. The pointe technique's

---

[31] The term 'sylph' refers to a mythological figure, also commonly designed as 'spirit of the air' (Barringer & Schlesinger, 2004).
[32] Au (1989).
[33] The French term 'tour de force' can be translated into 'feat'.

expressive potential was very present in movements such as the *pirouette*[34] or the *pas de bourrée couru*[35]. Thus, the movement *en pointe* developed from a mere stunt to a means of artistic expression and anchored itself deeply in dance technique; nowadays, the performance on the dancer's toes is an essential component of classic dance presentations. This way, it also influenced dance aesthetics: as the professional artists evolved technical feats which demanded a high degree of training and skill, the spectators' attention was increasingly directed from the complete stage design towards the dancer's body. In order to seize the complicated footwork of the romantic ballerinas, their long costumes were shortened as well as their opaque fabric was replaced by transparent, sleazy muslin[36]; the female dancer's *tutu*[37] was created.

However, the pointe shoe also has a very special impact on the dancer's body. Guiding the artist's movements in a proper way, the 'pointe technology' extends the body's repertoire of dance steps and allows it to progress in an unnatural but artistic manner. In the same time, one has to consider the fact that "the freedom to create such magic is rooted in the command of craft" (Barringer & Schlesinger, 2004:vii): the dancer has to adapt her body to the new technical feat by extensive physical work in order to incorporate the technology and achieve the effect of illusive weightlessness. Here, the dichotomic character of ballet becomes fragrant, as the ballerina's lightness and ease are the result of an immense amount of craft, discipline and physical power. Having understood this fact, one is certainly likely to agree with John Cranko explaining that "ballet may be the most physical of the performing arts, but it only becomes art when it appears as unphysical" [38] (Cranko,1974:31).

The pointe shoe not only forms the performing body through a special technique: fitting like a glove[39], it enables the body to exert movements which it could not exert autonomously. Extending the body's performance, it adapts a rather prosthetic function. In this context, it is also very interesting to note that even nowadays, professional dancers have a very intimate relationship to their dance shoes, and the attention they are according to their satin slippers

---

[34] A turn of the body done while standing on one leg, the other leg being held in any one of a number of traditional positions. A pirouette is done on demi-pointe by the male, on pointe by the female dancer.
[35] This is a progression on the points or demi-pointes by a series of small, even steps with the feet close together. It may be done in all directions or in a circle. Retrieved May 4, 2006 from http://www.abt.org/education/dictionary/terms/steps_ways.html
[36] Au, Susan (1988).
[37] The tutu is the short classical ballet skirt made of many layers of tarlatan or net. The romantic tutu is a long skirt reaching below the calf.
[38] "Ballett ist sicherlich das körperlichste unter den Bühnenfächern, aber es wird erst zur Kunst, wenn es unkörperlich wirkt"
[39] Barringer & Schlesinger (2004).

almost resembles extensive body care[40]. The close contact between the human corpus and this mundane technology can also be witnessed in the fact that the dance shoes also leave their traces on the dancer's body, as through a years-long training *en pointe* her footbones are modulated according to the form of her shoes (fig. 2.1, 2.2)[41].

 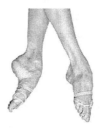

Figures 2.2, 2.3 (left to right): intensive work with pointe shoes visibly forms a dancer's feet

The technology of the pointe shoe engrained itself deeply into dance movement and its aesthetics, and the Romantic spirit reigning in 19th century's society was very conducive to its success. Its influence is considerable as nowadays, pointe dance is an essential choreographic element[42] and the tutu can be considered as a dancer's traditional costume. Furthermore, this mundane technology has come into very close contact with the dancer; its relation with the performing body is as intimate that the pointe shoe almost seems being part of the dancer's corpus. This fact is also underlined in currently presented classical dance performances as here, the application of the pointe technique is 'taken for granted': it has become an organic part of ballet technique and thus does not need to be explicitly demonstrated like in its experimental state during the epoch of Romanticism.

---

[40] The female dancer prepares each pair of pointe shoes herself before using it: according to her personal needs, she fixes the satin ribbons, softens or hardens the shoe soles and works on the hard toe box. This preparation process, which effectively has a ritual character can require several hours. (Barringer & Schlesinger, 2004).
[41] Barringer & Schlesinger (2004).
[42] ibid.

2.2 Video performance

Having invaded our lives, it was normal that sooner or later screens would end up invading our stages.[43]

Béatrice Picon-Vallin (1989:23)

Compared to the pointe shoe, the application of video technology's effect on dance is different insofar as it not only affects the concrete bodily performance but also extends the notions of presence, space and time. Or, as Béatrice Picon-Vallin explains when discussing the influence of video technology on theatre, "video can eventually show what is not presentable on stage" (Picon-Vallin, 1998:23)[44]. This chapter will give examples illustrating in how far an epochal technology such as video influenced the three basic elements of dance and emancipated from a sheer stage effect to an integrated part of the performance itself.

Derived from film technology, video was developed in the 1960s. With its continuous flow of electromagnetic signals, video technology not only allowed the instrumental recording of reality; it also gave place to "unlimited possibilities for image transformation and manipulation in the recording or post-production process" (Berghaus, 2005:183) and thus provided new possibilities to the performing arts[45]. Although its features know manifold applications in the domain of dance, such as video installations and video dance, I will concentrate here on video performance, that is (dance) performances integrating video projections on stage[46]. While in video dance and several installations, "the body serves as raw material (and) the movements are specially generated for the camera" (Berghaus, 2005:225), thus dance is made suitable to the technology[47], video performance is an illustration of how dance actively appropriates a technology.

In the epoch of 1960, video's predecessors such as photography and film had already engendered the image's increasing presence and social importance in daily life. Furthermore, the overall success of the audio-visual medium television raised general consciousness of the growing importance of representation technologies. These particular circumstances drove the performing arts not only to use, but also to reflect those media within their works[48]. This means that when

---

[43] "Les écrans ... ayant envahi nos vies, il était normal que, tôt ou tard, ils finissent par envahir nos scènes"

[44] "La vidéo peut enfin donner à voir ce qui n'est pas montrable sur un plateau"

[45] Evert (2003).

[46] Berghaus (2005).

[47] Video dance refers to the production of dance videos. Here, according to Berghaus, " the movements and movement sequences [are] composed in a manner determined by the image flow rather than by physical impulse" (Berghaus, 2005:223)

[48] Berghaus (2005).

present in (dance) performance, video technology is not only exploited as a means of expression but it is very often inspiring the choreography's creative theme. For example, the video performance significantly entitled *Muybridge – Man walking at ordinary speed*[49] of the Belgian choreographer Frédéric Flamand not only juxtaposes real dancers with their video projections on stage but also makes the mediated presence through video and photography its central idea. In the following text I will show whether and how the use of filmic devices on stage "has an effect on dance technique, the relation of the production's parameters to each other as well as on the choreographic treatment of space and the body's choreographic staging on the platform"[50] (Evert, 2003:44).

Günter Berghaus explains that in video performances "the discourse of the body is combined with the discourse of the medium. The juxtaposition of the two information systems allows the audience to compare and critically assess the two simultaneous presentations of an organic body and its artificial image" (Berghaus, 2005:184, see figs. 2.4, 2.5). In many cases, video performances using the projections of a dancer who is also physically present on stage, create a tension if not a competitive relation between the two bodies: the filmic body's characteristics differ from those of its referent, the first demonstrating superiority in diverse aspects. Not only the body's split presence is engendered through video technology, its segmentation too is allowed through "the camera's technical possibility to approach details with close-ups or to stretch motion sequences through slow motion"[51] (Evert, 2003:47). Thus, the dancer's body can be present(ed) in a manner differing from the conventional possibilities on stage. Furthermore, Günter Berghaus explains that "the camera lens creates views of the dancer's body that are impossible to experience in a theatre setting" (Berghaus, 2005:227-228), referring to the wide range of camera perspectives. The manipulation of video images also allows the filmic body to be freed of anatomical limits: for example, the filmic dancers in Flamand's *Muybridge – Man walking at ordinary speed* can jump higher and stay longer in the air than their 'real' counterparts and are able to (dis)appear without entering or leaving the stage. In this context, one has to be conscious of the fact that the technical features previously mentioned are part of a wider range of

---

[49] This title refers to the British photographer Eadweard Muybridge (1830-1904) whose studies of 'motion photography' represented the different moments of the body's movement. 'Man walking at ordinary speed' counts as one of Muybridge's most popular works.
[50] "Der Ansatz, filmische Verfahrensweisen auf Choreographie und Tanz zu übertragen, wirkt sich auch auf die Tanztechnik, das Verhältnis der Inszenierungsparameter zueinander sowie auf die choreographische Behandlung des Raumes und die choreographische Inszenierung des Körpers auf der Bühne aus"
[51] "… die Möglichkeiten der Kamera, Details in Großaufnahmen heranzuholen oder Bewegungsabläufe in der Zeitlupe zu dehnen"

possibilities and are still in the state of exploration; nevertheless, their inexhaustibility grows with every technical progress.

Figures 2.4, 2.5 (left to right): two possibilities of using video technology in stage performances, presented by the French company Mulleras

Even if video technology may possess an intangible because non-materialistic character, it has a direct influence on dance movements and their style. For example, in order to produce the images which later will be projected on stage, one has to consider the film camera's specificities. This means that the dancer's body has to be positioned in a manner which suits best to camera recording. As "the three-dimensional nature of space and of the dancer's body are not sufficiently seized" [52] (Evert, 2003: 40) by a video camera, the filmic body will explore movements which move in height and width rather than using a deep space because the screen's depth is very limited. Thus, the steps danced for video performance differ considerably from those effectuated in conventional stage productions. According to Kerstin Evert, the American choreographer Merce Cunningham made this experience during the rehearsals for his video performances: "the camera created changes in the daily training and in the dance technique: more work was effectuated with narrow foot positions. ... The jumps became higher and less space-taking" (Evert, 2003:53). Furthermore, as most video projections have oversized dimensions, the dancer is no longer dependent on expanding movements in order to capture the audience's attention. This is why dancers' steps in video performances are more limited on a spatial level and demonstrate more simplicity; the importance of technical virtuosity in classic dance has shifted to

---

[52] "Die Dreidimensinalität des Raumes und des Tänzerkörpers wird nicht ausreichend erfasst."

the mastering of complex rhythm patterns and the capacity to adapt one's movements to those presented via a screen[53].

However, video's influence on stage performances is not limited to its effects on the dancer and his movement as it is equally present on a spatio-temporal level. Here again, Picon-Vallin's already quoted statement "video can eventually show what is not presentable on stage" (1989:23) is of utmost actuality, as video performance questions the theatre's unity in space and time.

With its projection surface, video performance introduces a supplementary two-dimensional space to the three-dimensional stage. Mostly represented in the form of a screen, the projection surface extends the idea of space as it is able to overcome the stage's spatial constraints in referring to and presenting the space outside of the podium. In this sense, Frédéric Flamand for example projects various settings like city centres, streets or marketplaces on the dance platforms and thus lets his dancers move in and through those technologically represented settings. In his production *Live*, the Dutch choreographer Hans van Manen lets his dancers leave the stage at the moment of performance. With the help of a video camera, the artists are represented not only on stage but also in the space surrounding them, in this case the backstage area. In the context of a video performance, the idea of performance space as defined by the stage's size is extended and becomes an object of exploration. In playing with their possibilities and shifting the boundaries between exterior and interior, present and non-present space, choreographers clarify the effect of technical mediation.

The idea of splitting a previously existing unity is equally valid for the temporal aspect of a live performance. Video technology allowing the recordings' storage, one and the same sequence can be presented at will. In the context of a video performance, this means that the dancer's instantaneous movements are juxtaposed with the filmic body's pre-recorded performance, provided that the projection does not take place in real time. The recorded body enjoys a timeless existence: even if the moment of recording can be determined, the filmic body will not age like its original referent and its performance will not change in the slightest manner unless it is artificially modified. But video manipulation also allows the juxtaposition of different time levels. While the human body is constantly bound to its live presence, thus its performance in real time, the projected sequence can be presented in slow motion, in acceleration or simply pause in the middle of a jump. In this context, also a choreography's narrative structure can be altered, as cuts are possible at every moment and the change of dynamics and abrupt transitions

---

[53] Berghaus (2005).

can easily be effectuated[54]. For example, the performer usually necessarily entering and leaving the stage can be left out of the filmic choreography while it is always present in the performance happening on stage[55]. Video performance thus also allows to show up and explore the tension between direct and recorded performance.

Although video performance will always have an experimental character in trying to catch up with the latest technical progress, video technology's influence on stage is visible in different aspects. On the one hand, "the special demands created through the production with a camera influences dance technique and its training in order to prepare the [dancers'] physical work for the medium's specificities"[56] (Evert, 2003:53). On the other, the used recording technology questions the performance's 'here and now' and thus plays with the idea of temporal and spatial presence which has been hitherto understood as one of theatre's "fundamental elements" (Evert, 2003:155). In this sense, video technology has become a part of this particular type of theatrical dance which uses video in a self-referential way. Nowadays, the qualitative difference between live and mediated is emphasised by digital video technology allowing live projections without any perceptible temporal shift. With the help of video technology, the body as well as its movement start generating the choreography's idea on their own and thus join the stream of modern dance which emphasises the telling of movement rather than narrating a story[57]. This idea contrasts with the concept of the balletic, classical body[58] which is "mimetic and [therefore] not producing sense in itself"[59] (Vila, 1998:32).

Furthermore, this section has made clear that the relation between the dancer and video differs considerably from the engagement linking the human body to the mundane technology of the pointe shoe. As in pointe dance, the dance shoe adopts a prosthetic function through its direct physical contact with the dancer, the performing body 'digests' the technology to the point that the satin slippers almost appear as a part of the dancer herself. Video dance on the contrary requires a projection surface, mostly represented by a screen, because it is only with the help of this interface that the contact between dancer and video technology can be established. Therefore, the relation between performer and technology gains a more abstract character.

---

[54] Berghaus (2005).
[55] Picon-Vallin (1998).
[56] "Die besonderen Anforderungen, die durch eine Kameraproduktion entstehen, schlagen sich in Tanztechnik und – training nieder, um die Tänzer in der täglichen Körperarbeit auf die Anforderungen des Mediums vorzubereiten."
[57] Vila (1998).
[58] In most classic choreographies, the dancer's body is supposed to imitate the characters of a story but also animals like in *Swan Lake* or fantastic creatures such as sylphs or elves.
[59] "Le corps classique est mimétique et ainsi non pas producteur en lui-même du sens."

Nevertheless, also here both components are closely connected as the recorded video image is based and thus depends on a referent, which in this case is the dancer's body; the projected video image is thus "related and at the same time independent from the life of the 'real' body" (Portanova, 2005). Moreover, it is precisely the play and interaction between the dancer and his recorded image which gives sense to the performer's movement and both bodies' presence on stage. Although video performance may appear more abstract as it introduces a certain distance to the human body which is even reinforced by the option of post-recording modification, video technology influences the dancer's performance. Thus, even though it does not adopt a prosthetic function, video represents a technology to the body as it makes the dancer learn to perform in a new manner.

Contrary to the pointe shoe which was specially created for dance performance, dance's integration of video also illustrates the performing art form's capacity to appropriate a technology which was originally designed for other purposes. Thus, dance anticipated video's primal aim as a pure representation technology.

2.3 Multimedia performance

> *Recent advances in computing ... are fundamentally changing the way many dance artists create [and] present their work.*

De Spain (2000:3)

Like video, computer technologies too have been applied early in the field of dance. In this context, it is notable that dance did not hesitate to appropriate New Media in various domains. Thus, nowadays almost all current dance performances make use of computerised stage technology, such as for the control of the stage box or for lighting[60]. Furthermore, computer technologies revealed themselves as effective means for dance notation[61] as well as for choreography[62], and *Improvisation Technologies*, a software designed by the American choreographer William Forsythe, is an interactive dancing school developed for educational purposes.

---

[60] Evert (2003).
[61] Dance notation refers to the act of fixing movement in writing.
[62] One example for choreographic creation on a computer is the software *Life Forms* (retrieved May 18, 2006, from http://www.charactermotion.com).

Closely tied to the societal circumstances embedding its performance and with its openness to the emerging technologies of its relative epochs, dance also started early to appropriate, use and reflect New Technologies in live multimedia performances. With the constant technical progress, computer technologies' possibilities increased and are still being improved. Thus, multimedia performance remains an actual phenomenon as the process of the technologies' exploration is far from being concluded. However, like already mentioned in the introduction of this thesis, the disembodying effect of New Technologies engenders "formal disjunctions between properties of the digital and the essential components of dance practice involving human motion, corporeality and physical presence" (DeLahunta, 2002:66); the combination of New Media and the dancing body might appear contradictory.

In this section I will briefly situate New Technologies in their societal context and present digitalisation's consequences on (the actual image of) the human body in order to investigate whether computer technologies may appear incompatible with dance performance or even menace it from its status as a "physical art" (Cranko, 1979:33). As the technologies used in contemporary dance productions are various and often still in the state of exploration, the subsequent section (2.3.2) will present a concrete example of New Technologies which has already been repeatedly applied during stage performances, namely the principle of *Motion Capturing*. Seizing human movement and transmitting it on computer-generated forms and figures, this technology joins the idea of the body's disappearance through digitalisation and thus qualifies as an appropriate example.

2.3.1 New Technologies and body discourse

"Computerisation affects deeper and deeper layers of culture", says Lev Manovich when introducing *The Language of New Media* (Manovich, 2001:27), making allusion to New Technologies' undeniable status as an epochal and thus cultural technology. This means that their impact and importance transcend New Media's role as pure means for information processing as they are actually "[transforming] our view of the world and our body image" (Dinkla, 2002), shaping the identity of post-modern culture[63]. New Technologies (NT) being applied in various domains, their influence on current social and cultural patterns reveals an utmost complexity[64]. In

---

[63] Dinkla (2002).
[64] Here, it is not only the question of New Technologies' influence on our changed perception of distance and time, as for example the Internet enables us to 'reach' a very distant location within several seconds. The technologies

this context, the effect of disembodiment attributed to computers' abstract processing with digital data is certainly one of NT's most contended effects.

The 'digital era' is anchored in a society in which the human body seems "colonized by technology" (Berghaus, 2005:51), as high scientific progress attributes an almost replaceable character to the organic corpus. Advances in the field of biotechnology for example do not only allow the production of technological implants replacing organs of the human body, but also the artificial reproduction of (human) beings is made possible. Thus, one of Man's most human properties can, at least theoretically, be imitated by technical products. Furthermore, technology's superiority is demonstrated as current scientists are even able to modify living beings in their prenatal stage. Here, the organic body appears subject to and mastered by technological power and becomes increasingly transparent through medical examination. However, the rising importance and reign of (new) technology becomes also clear in a more general context, as already in nowadays' steadily growing computerised work processes "the body loses its importance as tasks can be assumed by [computer] machines or specialised industrial robots. Humans and their bodies seem to be superfluous"[65] (Evert, 2003:16-17). In this context, the human being as well as its body gain an obsolete character as they are too fallible to keep up with computational power.

As already suggested, New Technologies' influence on objective reality and the human corpus is partly due to their digital processing, that is the representation of objects or New Media products with the help of numerical coding[66]. This means that each object appearing on a computer screen is described formally, for instance through the application of algorithms or mathematical functions. The process of digitalisation thus signifies the translation of objects and bodies into abstract data. In order to enter this mathematical system, the human body too has to undergo a transformation into measurable categories and numbers[67]. This procedure does not only attach mathematical dimensions to the body but also translates it into a system in which "the stored or processed information has no corporeal existence, and no intrinsic material alliance is formed between message and carrier" (Berghaus, 2005:236). Furthermore, a digitised representation "consists of independent parts, each of which consists of smaller independent parts, and so forth, down to the level of the smallest 'atoms' – [the] pixels" (Manovich, 2001:31); here, at its base

---

emerging are also introducing new social practices, as for example socialising nowadays can take place in online chat rooms and it is possible to search for a partner on virtual dating sites.

[65] "... der Körper [verliert] zusehends an Bedeutung, da Aufgaben von [Computer] Maschinen [...] übernommen werden."

[66] Manovich (2001).

[67] For example, specific criteria of the body's measurement serve for a realistic computerised representation of the body.

the body does not appear as a unity anymore but is fragmented. Although the idea of the body's decomposition through representation technologies has already been introduced by the photographic camera[68], digital technology further allows the independent modification of each element and thus renders it programmable[69]. It is precisely its numerical representation, hardly showing any traces of materiality and substance which provokes a discussion about the body's role and future in a society of increasing digitalisation[70], as NT's analytic principle provides new possibilities but in the same time provokes the fear of the body's disappearance through technological hegemony.

Nevertheless, the digitalisation process does not only 'decompose' existing objects in their representation; it also demonstrates synthetic qualities as it allows the creation of virtual environments commonly referred to as *Virtual Reality* (VR). VR thus stands for the numerical creation of spaces which are merely consisting of programmed data sets. Although these artificially created environments are materially non-existing, users can enter these realistic but unreal worlds with the help of head-mounted displays[71] or data gloves[72]. These specific devices are supposed to make the user's (mental) immersion into virtual cyberspace possible, enabling him to experience another reality. Applications in the domain of VR thus aim at a simulation which is almost identical to reality itself[73], or as Dirk Vaihinger puts it: "Virtuality is the objective world promising to be reality without having to be it"[74] (1997:21). Consequently, "in a digital environment, the referent for a text or image is no longer an objective reality, but concepts of reality" (Berghaus, 2005:72). In this context, Berghaus further argues that with the growing presence of VR, the boundaries between reality and simulation become increasingly blurred (2005). This aspect distinguishes the technology of VR with the already mentioned technologies of the pointe shoe and video. While the pointe shoe has become an instrument to, and almost of, the body, video aims at the representation of reality and the body, but it does never join the idea of simulation. Here it becomes visible that the dancing shoes as well as video are tightly bound

---

[68] It is the practice of motion photography, developed in the early 20th century by the photographers Etienne-Jules Marey and Eadweard Muybridge which allows the fragmented recording of human and animal motion.

[69] Manovich (2001).

[70] Evert (2003).

[71] The head-mounted display (HMD) is "a graphical display device, such as a pair of tiny LCD screens worn like goggles. Often combined in a single helmet with position tracking sensors and earphones for 3-D sound" (retrieved June 2nd, 2006, from http://www.hitl.washington.edu/scivw/EVE/IV.Definitions.html).

[72] Data gloves are "equipped with sensors that sense the movements of the hand and interfaces those movements with a computer" (retrieved June 2nd, 2006, from http://www.webopedia.com/TERM/D/data_glove.htm).

[73] Here, also the original significance of the term 'virtual' is of interest, as it designs the idea of "being such in essence or effect though not in actual fact" (retrieved May 13, 2006 from http://www.wordreference.com/definition/virtual).

[74] "Virtualität ist die Objektwelt, die Wirklichkeit zu sein verspricht, ohne sie sein zu müssen."

to, and in a certain way dependent on the human body while New Technologies seem to decompose and simulate it. Nevertheless, I already explained that in a certain sense, also the pointe shoe and video rudimentarily lead to a confusion between technology and the dancer's corpus, as the dance shoe achieves a prosthetic status and a performer's projected video image also has a given presence on stage. However, while these two technologies rely on the dancer's body and are actively appropriated by the artist, the digitalisation process rather seems to digest the organic body itself.

The rising confusion between the object and its (virtual) representation is especially present in the actual discourse around the body, as digitalisation's binary code also allows the creation of virtual figures which are quasi identical to their living referents. One example is certainly NT's influence on physical aesthetics, as the highly stylised, almost unnatural physical ideal of simulated bodies in the domain of entertainment, such as virtual television animators or the heroes of computer games, appear to affect the visual criteria of real, organic bodies[75]. But digitalisation's 'benefits' even reach so far as nowadays corpuses translated into 'zeros and ones'[76] serve as models for virtual surgery, i.e. the computational simulation of medical operation[77]. Here, the digital image is likely to replace the original body.

The substitution of the body by its image and the latter's steadily growing importance, strengthened by the use of New Technologies, provokes polemic discourses about the human's waning presence and corporeality. In this context, the contemporary philosopher Jean Baudrillard declares (new) media as simulation machines which reproduce images, signs and codes constituting an autonomous realm of reality, which he designs as "hyperreality" (Baudrillard, 1994:68). According to the French theorist, the existing world is no longer in touch with New Technologies' (re)productions; the real is even subordinate to its abstract representation and we are consequently living in a world of signs. In this sense, we tend for example to consider images of an object in the same manner in which we would look at the object itself. For Baudrillard, this effect has an utmost pejorative character, as it signifies the end of reality: "there is no place for the world and its double" (Baudrillard, 1997:27). Abstraction and dematerialisation engendering the loss of corporeality are also a theme in Paul Virilio's works. In his *Aesthetics of disappearance*, he declares that "soon we can only forget that there still exist subtle differences between the diffusion of images [on the one hand] and objects and bodies [on the other]" (Virilio,

---

[75] For example the figure of Lara Croft, the virtual heroine of the computer game *Tomb Raider*, inspires women all over the world to participate in 'Lara look-alike' events and webpages. See for example www.planetlara.com (retrieved June 2nd, 2006).
[76] This expression refers to digitalisation's binumerical code.
[77] Székely (1999).

1986:83) when discussing the impact of digitalisation. Virilio designs computer technologies as "the last vehicle", accusing in his homonymous essay the speed of information processing to deprive human beings from their physical and sensory experience[78]. According to Virilio, the arrival of New Technologies resembles "the advent of a final generation of vehicles, ... a static vehicle, substitute for the change of physical location, ... a vehicle that ought at last to bring about the victory of ... an ultimate sedentariness" (quoted in Redhead, 2004:112). In their argumentations, both philosophers present New Technologies as a menace to the physical presence of objects and bodies and predict their replacement by (virtual) simulations. This reasoning leads to the idea that computer technologies' abstract proceeding engenders a more conceptual view of the world, implicating the confusion of the original with its representation. Furthermore, Virilio argues that the use of NT can be equated with the human body's amputation, rendering it into a paralysed, because motionless, organism. Here, "virtual existence ... [seems] constituted through discourses that are firmly rooted in a body-hostile culture" (Berghaus, 2005:249).

This perspective seems to offend dance as an art which is bound to the body's presence and raises the question whether the increasing mediatisation is also affecting and taking over the 'live' body present in the 'here and now' of theatrical performance. This context raises the question whether the human performer might one day be substituted by a synthetic, digital dancer. Considering this apparent incongruence with dance[79], (how) can NT effectively be integrated into dance performance? And how can a relation between the performer's body and computer technologies be established? In order to clarify the consequences of NT application in the context of physical performance, I will now present the technology of Motion Capturing.

---

[78] Redhead (2004).
[79] In this context, Jacques de Vroomen refers to the incoherency of theatrical multimedia performances: "[Nieuwe] Media en theater zijn als olie en water. Als je ze bij elkaar voegt en je schudt ze stevig dan lijkt het bij eerste oogopslag een aardige mix. Kijk je iets langer dan zie je een deel water en een deel olie. Van een vermenging of integratie is geen sprake... Enerzijds zijn er de spelers, de dansers van vlees en bloed tegenover het geprojecteerde plaatje" (De Vroomen, 2001:17).

2.3.2 The principle of digitalised movement: Motion Capturing

This new way of looking at movement material ... will influence the art of making dances.

Scott deLahunta (2000)

Since the 1980's, Motion Capturing alias *Mocap* is used for the digital recording of movement[80]. Particularly applied in the entertainment industry and more precisely in the context of trick films, the technology renders the movement of animated characters as realistic as possible. This is due to the fact that, other than in film and video, not the image of the moving (human) body but exclusively its movement is recorded[81]: entered into a computer and digitalised, it can for example be converted to trick figures. Nowadays, a growing number of dance companies are integrating Motion Capturing into their works. The increasing interest in this technology is certainly due to the manifold possibilities it proposes, allowing to reflect the impact of New Technologies on the human body in diverse ways.

The process of Motion Capturing knows different input devices enabling the computer to seize the body's movement. A very common means is the dancer wearing a suit equipped with magnetic sensors which are placed at selected points of the body, for example at the joints, the head and the hip. In this case, the body's connection to the computer via cables allows the transmission of its movement data (fig. 2.6). Another possibility is the optical *Mocap* system: here, infrared-reflecting sensors are fixed on strategic points of the body[82] (fig. 2.7). The sensors' reflections are captured by one or mostly several cameras and then delivered to the computer which "interprets the sensors as a set of points moving in relation to each other" (Evert, 2003:75). As already mentioned, once 'digested' by the

Figure 2.6: a dancer demonstrating the suit for magnetic motion capture

computer, the body's movement is played back in a three-dimensional digital space and converted to computer-generated human and non-human figures. In the context of dance

---

[80] deLahunta (2000).
[81] Evert (2003).
[82] Scott deLahunta reports that the most strategic body parts in optical Motion Capture are the head, shoulders, elbows, wrists, knees and ankles while three points are moving down the spine (deLahunta, 2000).

performances, those moving images are commonly projected on a screen present on stage. For example, in Merce Cunningham's 1999 creation *Biped*, the dancers are performing with figures consisting of several lines, making only slight allusions to body forms (fig. 2.8). These merely conceptual figures execute the dancers' same movements; thus, as deLahunta formulates it: "What you see ... is a series of abstract shapes which are animated with human movement" (2000). Motion being reduced to the sensors' animation in the *Mocap* process, it gains a dematerialised character and seems abstracted from the dancer's body. Here, dance appears separated from its origin, the dancer's corpus; the digital recordings are likely to represent "a

form of 'pure motion', freed from the physical figure of the performer" (Evert, 2003:77), uniquely presented by the projection's bundles of light rays.

Furthermore, the *Mocap* principle transcends its capacity of the sheer transmission of human dance on computer-generated forms, as once the dancer's movement is digitalised it can be subject to modification. Such is for instance the case in *Biped*: although the performance of the virtual figures is

Figure 2.7: optical motion capture works with infrared-reflecting sensors

based on steps effectuated by the choreography's dancers, the line-drawn forms are presenting the same movements but in miscellaneous, mixed-up sequences which are numerically altered. The possibilities of digital manipulation are nowadays reaching so far that movement can even be split into different data sets. For example, due to its relatively high cost, some artists possess technological equipment with a reduced number of sensors. While this does not cause any problems in the virtualisation of simple exercises, it can reveal as more problematic in the case of complex steps requiring the activity of many body parts. Here, it is possible to divide the motion sequence and join the different parts after the recording[83]. However, it is obvious that this modification process still relies on the performance of a 'real' body.

---

[83] The performer and choreographer Scott deLahunta thus reports from the preparatory work for one of his creations: "because there were only seven sensors, all of the material was captured twice, once with the sensors placed on the

Figure 2.8:
Motion capture allows
the animation of virtual
forms in Merce
Cunningham's 'Biped'

The possibilities of Motion Capturing are not limited to the exclusive reproduction of dancing steps as the technology also enables movement to trigger diverse effects on stage: with the help of different software programs, the motion data "can be used to control a variety of media [such as] sound, lights, [and] music"[84]. For example, the German dance company *Mouvoir* under the direction of the choreographer Stephanie Thiersch uses this technology in diverse productions. In the creation *Wunderland* ('Wonderland') which is composed for one dancer, the performer's movement triggers sound effects as well as the projection of images and colours on the dance floor. Thus, the artist seems for instance to be followed by virtual lines which are changing colours or appear and disappear according to her movement. While in *Wunderland*, the dancer's entire body is triggering the stage effects, specific sensors in the form of electrodes[85] even allow the recording and transformation of body movements hitherto unknown to stage performance, such as brainwaves, muscle activity and heartbeat. This way, it is "possible to pick up the [movement] generated by individual muscle groups, [convert] the signals ... and thus allow them to be used to control diverse stage effects"[86]. This process is applied in Thiersch's creation entitled *ba:ab*, where the brainwaves of one dancer trigger the projection of diverse images on a screen which in their turn influence the dancers' performance. The projection's order being

---

upper torso ... and once again with the sensors placed on the lower part of the body.... The two data sets were then assembled together, one on top of the other" (deLahunta, 2000).
[84] The quotation is retrieved from the homepage of the dance company *Palindrome* which is specialised in the application of NT in dance performance (retrieved June 5, 2006, from http://www.palindrome.de).
[85] "Electrodes are small electrically-conductive pads or strips which, when pressed or glued to the skin, allow movements from within the body to be detected" (retrieved June 5, 2006, from http://www.palindrome.de).
[86] retrieved June 5, 2006, from http://www.palindrome.de

dependent on the flow of brainwaves, the image sequence is unpredictable and so is the choreographic development of each performance.

The presented examples show that the process of Motion Capturing allows the virtualisation of human movement. In this context, the technology seems to join the idea of disembodiment discussed in the previous chapter: the movement's abstraction from the human body and its transformation into programmable units draws clear parallels to the body's fragmentation into pixels during the digitalisation process. Furthermore, the dancer's agitation does not only appear as 'decomposed' through motion capture as it is also likely to emancipate from its original source in two senses. On the one hand, it is liberated from the material of the organic corpus which until now was intimately connected, if not considered as necessary for the generation of movement in dance. On the other hand, the post-recording process allowing its modification, movement emancipates in developing its form outside of the human body. Its abstraction and alienation seems to hit its peak during the dance steps' transformation into the triggering of different stage effects. Also here, the body gains an obsolete character as its status as the medium of motion is questioned through technology. Tying up with Virilio's theory, the dancer's direct physical attachment to the computer via sensors and cables may appear as the body's amputation because technology's direct impact on dance performance reveals itself as highly constrictive[87]. During the very process of motion capture, the technology is closely tied to the human body as their physical contact is established by the dancer wearing either a special suit or reflecting sensors. This proximity seems to disappear when the performer's movement is transmitted onto another virtual body or even modified; here the technology takes a distance to the human corpus and even appears to demonstrate the latter's redundancy. In rendering it obsolete, *Mocap* represents a danger to the human body; the corpus' engagement with technology takes a self-destructive character.

Although Motion Capturing demonstrates that the (re)presentation of movement is not imperatively tied to the human body, this technology is far from depriving neither dance nor its

---

[87] Although the process of Motion Capturing aims at recording movement without constraints, it affects and influences dance performance. It is already through the sensors' fixation on the performer's body as well as the multiple cables of the magnetic *Mocap* process that some dancers may experience constraints in their freedom of movement; this sensation can indeed affect their dancing style (Leeker, 2002). Furthermore, magnetic Motion Capturing does not only constrict the choreography's possibilities through transmission cables as the performance can only be effectuated inside of the magnetic field necessary for this form of recording. While optical Motion Capture allows more freedom to the performing body, its infrared reflections can be easily masked during complex exercises or the work with a partner (deLahunta, 2000). As the captivated movement is interrupted when occluded, the dancer must respect the technology's specificity in exclusively effectuating the kind of steps allowing the sensors' visibility. Consequently, the performance of *pirouettes* and complex floor work finds itself excluded from the dancer's vocabulary.

dancer from their corporeal aspects. Even if at first, it might appear restrictive to the dancer, the *Mocap* process allows the manifestation and reflection of a new body image in dance performance and acknowledges a new role to the dancer's corpus. In presenting the human body as a fragmented form which can be separated from its movement and challenged by virtual forms and figures, *Mocap*-animated dance performances are adjusting the dancer's presentation to the decomposed body concept reigning in the digital era. This effect is underlined by the use of electrodes capturing the dancer's inner movements, as here also the current medical view of the human body is introduced into dance aesthetics. In this context, Stephanie Thiersch states that "dance is a reflection of reality, of our reality", explaining that "the use of technologies on stage is but a reaction of the exterior circumstances"[88]. In this perspective, the technology of Motion Capturing represents a means of expression for dance, enabling the performing art to present and reflect the reality it is embedded in.

Furthermore, the process of Motion Capturing does not only restrict the dancer's performance as it also enables him to influence and act upon the virtual realm presented on screen without the use of a helmet or gloves: the device mediating between real and virtual, man and mechanical construct is the combination of the dancer's body and the computer-connected sensors. Thus, the body is likely to represent an interface on its own, establishing the contact with virtual figures or computer-generated stage effects through its movement. Here, corporeal existence gains a quasi essential character, as "it is through flesh and not in spite of it that [the dancer] gains access to the virtual"[89] (Kozel, 1994:37). The necessity of physical presence in this context represents a clear argument against the idea of dematerialisation through New Technologies, as the latter put a new focus on the "exploration of the body as an instrument of dynamic movement" (Dinkla, 2002). Moreover, the technology enables the dancer to let his movement transcend his kinaesthetic reach because his body triggers effects in virtual space or directly on stage; *Mocap* thus allows the artist to act upon his spatial surroundings. This capacity also acknowledges a certain control and thus power to the performer, because "the animation is driven by the dancer wearing the sensors" (deLahunta, 2000). This effect is especially visible in the context of Motion Capturing in real time, i.e. the transmission of movement without previous recording and modification. Besides the fact that this live proceeding reinforces the notion of immediacy in theatrical performance[90] as well as its form[91], the dancer's possibilities reach so far that he can

---

[88] Stephanie Thiersch's quotations result from a telephonic interview effectuated on May 20, 2006.
[89] The quotation is underlined in the original text.

[90] Although theatrical performance seems bound to the 'here and now', several stage effects are previously programmed. This is not the case when the actors are triggering those effects in the real time of the performance.

even influence the choreography itself. Such is the case in Stephanie Thiersch's *ba:ab*, as the brainwaves produced by one dancer are engendering the effects deciding about the piece's choreographic development. In this perspective, the used technology cannot be considered as a restrictive element anymore but rather adopts a prosthetic function, enabling the performing body to transcend in a certain way its anatomical limits. Here, the technological extension of the physical reach leads to the idea of Motion Capturing as a body technology.

I already suggested that the dancer's corpus is learned and mechanised and thus represents an instrument in itself (chapter 1.2). As the dancer has to adapt his body's functioning in order to work with *Mocap*, he makes it a technology to and of his body. Suddenly being able to influence his surroundings, the performer must learn to master new parameters which are extrinsic to his own corpus and seize their relation to his physical performance. In this context, Martina Leeker explains that many dancers encounter difficulties when applying the *Mocap* process for the first time. According to the German researcher, dancers feel "absorbed and overwhelmed by the amount of possibilities, but also by the power and the responsibility" (Leeker, 2002:242); the learned body thus has to re-learn in order to use the technology in an efficient way. Furthermore, this necessary process can reveal itself as very tedious[92]. Here, it becomes clear that the use of New Technologies affects the dancer's physical experience, or as Stephanie Thiersch puts it: "you discover and learn your body anew". Thus, the dancer's concrete confrontation with the effects of computer technology lead him back to a conscious examination and exploration of his body's possibilities as he has to reformulate its functioning.

The example of Motion Capturing presents the manifold possibilities offered by the use of New Media on dance stages. In this context, it is notable that although the process of digitalisation affects the dancer's body as well as its movement in liberating the latter from its original corpus, it proposes new directions to dance performance rather than constraining it or leading to a disembodied spectacle. More precisely, Söke Dinkla explains that "the strength of digital dance[93] lies in the ability ... to create a new perceptual space based on a transformed image of the human body" (Dinkla, 2002:24). True to its cultural circumstances, the Motion Capturing process allows dance to reflect the phenomenon of technological advance, (virtual) representation and the

---

[91] In this context, Stephanie Thiersch explains that "quite often, movements are only effectuated in order to achieve a certain technical effect [and that] instead of pausing from time to time, dancers don't stop moving because it's them who are triggering the stage effects".

[92] Evert (2003).

[93] Dinkla defines digital dance as "dance that views digital technologies as an integral component of the artistic process and as conveyors of a new physical self-image" (Dinkla,2002:20).

resulting body image in its proper manner, attaching contemporary characteristics to the performing body. Here, it becomes clear that once again, dance integrates and appropriates New Technology, giving way to a symbiotic relation with New Technologies instead of creating a problematic co-existence as predicted by Baudrillard. Also according to Dinkla, multimedia performances are "exploiting the aesthetic potential of the digital and the expressive power of the human body without winding up in the end of irreconcilable dichotomies" (Dinkla, 2002:24). While the use of NT influences the performing act as well as its form, the dancer's body is not likely to disappear in a multimedia performance because its status as the generator of movement cannot be challenged by the technology of Motion Capturing. Here, it becomes obvious that after its dissociation from the human body, the technology returns to the performer as it affects his learning and performance.

This chapter has demonstrated in how far different technologies such as the pointe shoe, video and the digital Motion Capturing have been appropriated to the characteristics of dance art but also inscribed themselves in its aesthetics and performance on several levels. Thus, each technology involved became an integral part of dance performance and influenced the presentation (of the human body) on stage. While the relation between the dancer's corpus and the technology of the pointe shoe or video demonstrates the latter's dependence on the human body, New Technologies such as Motion Capturing appear more distant as they seem to emancipate from the dancer. Nevertheless, also *Mocap* is based on the performer's movement and a closer look at the performer's engagement with this technology reveals that it also serves as an instrument to the human body in providing it with new possibilities. This finding underlines the relation between human and computer technology, demonstrating that their connection, and not their apparent dichotomy, are of importance.

While Motion Capturing is still based on the human component of motion, the next chapter introduces *Double Cue*, a creation of the French choreographer Patrice Barthès. In this dance piece, Barthès performs with a computationally created and animated figure. (How) can a relation between the dancer's organic body and an apparently completely artificial figure be established?

3. *Double Cue* : physical and virtual performance united

Although the technologies mentioned in the previous chapter affected dance performance on different levels, they all were directly tied or referring to a dancer's moving body. In this context, even the process of Motion Capturing could not challenge the dancer's status as a source of movement. This aspect seems to change through the use of animation software which not only allows the creation but also the artificial animation of virtual bodies. Here, the dancer's presence and role appear to be questioned anew as not only his body but the performer's movement too is generated by algorithmic calculation. Such is also the case in the 2004 creation *Double Cue* by the French choreographer Patrice Barthès: in this piece, the dancer's performance is accompanied by a virtual figure created with the animation software *Poser*[94]. As its movement is the result of data processing and not due to a dancer's dynamism, the virtual figure seems to be completely detached from any human element or presence. Hence, this idea might rise doubts on the human body's necessity. Is the programmable virtual figure likely to represent a 'perfect dancer' superior to an organic interpreter? Moreover, this same thought may also give rise to the question if a synthetic figure's motion can still be considered as dance art.

To what extent do dance performance and its aesthetics allow a relation between the organic body and an (apparently) purely synthetic figure? And how can a dancer get 'in touch' and perform with a seemingly ethereal, virtual partner? In presenting the case of *Double Cue*, I will try to analyse the impact of *Poser*'s use in dance performance and see in which way this software inscribes itself into the creative process as well as in the dancing body.

3.1 New Technologies, a creative inspiration

As already mentioned in the context of video application in dance (chapter 2.2), the use of representation technologies in stage choreographies does not only influence the works' concrete performance but also contributes to their main themes, often reflecting (mediated) representation and the increasing presence of technology in our lives. Also in the case of *Double Cue*, New Technologies are part of the choreography's creative idea.

---

[94] For more information on the software see ch. 3.3.

Patrice Barthès, French dancer and choreographer residing at Montpellier in Southern France is an independent creator since 1992. Although his work distinguishes itself through an experimental and innovative character, *Double Cue* is Barthès' first production integrating a computer program. It was notably a workshop dealing with the topic of solo dance which made the artist reflect about the notions of presence and absence in performance. In a spectacle following this workshop, the dancer chose not to appear on stage, as "to be absent is also a manner to 'be there'"[95]. Instead, Barthès' place was occupied by a virtual figure that possessed the dancer's morphology and performed his movements in a looped, thus repetitive sequence. "I did not know about this and was only told about the virtual projection later ... but what was really striking to me was the fact that for the audience, I had been present on stage. Even my three-year old son was saying about this projection that it was 'dad who was dancing'."

How can human presence be challenged by a virtual figure? And to what extent is software able to create dance movement? Inspired by his 'digital presence', Barthès decided to create an experimental choreography in confronting himself with a virtual image. "I wanted to meet the challenge of seeing how a virtual body, which in its form resembles the least to a human being[96] is able to perform dance movements and be part of a dance performance", the artist explains. "Then, in confronting myself with this figure which is nothing but 'zeros and ones', I wanted to find out if it can even affect my own presence or performance"[97]. From Barthès' quotation it becomes clear that the theme of *Double Cue* is based on the difference between reality and virtual spheres, manifested through the search of dance aesthetics in synthetic movement as well as its impact on a human dancer. It is already the work's title, referring to a 'dual prompt' which makes allusion to the two distinct sources of movement, namely the dancer and his virtual partner. In this context, it becomes obvious that the used technology is an integral part of Barthès' creation, as the circumstances driving the artist to create *Double Cue* demonstrate that New Technologies, in this case the (indirect) experience with his virtual projection, represent an essential inspiration for the choreographer. Furthermore, as the piece's creative theme relies on the work with synthetic movement, digital technology represents an essential part of the choreographic artwork.

So how does Barthès integrate the software *Poser* and its digitally created figure in his performance?

---

[95] Patrice Barthès' quotations are the result of interviews held during my fieldwork at Montpellier from April 22 until April 25, 2006.
[96] The virtual figure performing in *Double Cue* is wire-framed and thus, according to Barthès, merely resembles a human body's "envelope, a concept".
[97] NB: Barthès interprets his own creation.

3.2 The choreography *Double Cue*

Although conceived for one dancer, each presentation of *Double Cue* demands the contribution of four artists, as besides the performer, also a multimedia specialist is necessary for the virtual figure's projection. Furthermore, the piece's music is generated by the live play of a double-bass musician whose performance is simultaneously transformed with the help of computational means by a sound artist.

As I already suggested, Barthès' creation tells about the interplay between a dancer and his virtual double. During its length of approximately forty minutes, the choreography presents the gradual approach of the two performing bodies: if in the piece's beginning, Barthès as well as his synthetic counterpart manifest their different natures, both 'dancers' end up in a virtual *pas de deux. Double Cue*'s rhythm is created through the different stages marked by the two bodies' gradual approach as well as through two solo sequences in which Patrice Barthès or his virtual partner performs alone.

The choreography's opening presents a simple scenery: the sombre and undecorated stage is separated from the audience through a layer of transparent tulle that is hardly visible in the gloomy lighting. On the stage's centre, Patrice Barthès is stretched on the ground, lying on his right side and presenting his back to the audience; the dancer is exclusively clad in blue cotton trousers. His body is not entirely visible, as the stage lighting does not focus on a central spot but is divided into diverse light spots of varying sizes. Slowly but constantly moving, the lighting creates a rather fragmented view of the dancer's body. Also the double-bass player sitting on the stage's exterior left area is only partly visible, as her trunk is left in the dark. This effect makes the audience only see her instrument as well as her playing arms.

Barthès effectuates his first movements in lying on the dance floor; his slow and fluid performance demonstrates a visible attraction to the ground. He starts turning his body on the floor, moves his head but also his legs into the ceiling's direction without lifting himself entirely up. The dancer's slow movements, consisting of multiple stretchings and contractions, make the tension within his body generated by muscular work, highly visible. In an overall perspective, Barthès' performance demonstrates a fluid dynamic which is oriented in continuity and development rather than in the achievement of certain poses. The artist appears deeply immersed in his dance: without orienting his view to the audience, and sometimes even moving with his eyes closed, the dancer seems to concentrate exclusively on his body. Although fluid in character, Barthès' movements are visually fragmented through the multiple light spots, and his limbs are caught in a play of disappearance in and reappearance out of the stage's dark shadows. Until now, the dancer's performance is exclusively accompanied by computationally transformed, indefinable sounds.

In this sequence, Barthès manifests his human nature as his dance underlines the characteristics of an organic body. His movements on the ground suggest the body's attraction by gravity as well as the fluidity inherent to human motion. This impression is reinforced through the fact that turns and jumps are completely excluded of Barthès' vocabulary; those steps represent "a means which has always been used in dance for the overcoming of gravity"[98] (Evert, 2003:79). Furthermore, the body's half-nakedness renders Barthès' muscular work visible and thus once more focuses the spectator's attention on the dancer's organic nature.

It is when the virtualised sounds get louder and become more intensive that a first projection appears on the tulle fabric: a simple blue line resembling a laser beam traverses the stage's space, wandering from the floor up to the ceiling. While Barthès continues dancing, now several lines are projected on the transparent screen[99]. Slowly, their shapeless combination concretises in moulding a grid-like shape. As the virtual grid is taking the stage's overall space, the dancer's body seems to be caught in a spider web. In evolving, the grid's density increases and gives way to a pulsating, still indefinable form unless it suddenly develops into a human shape: a wire-framed figure appears on stage. The virtual body 'enters' the stage in flying. While the human dancer is now repeating one single sequence of movements whose only alteration consists in a change of directions, the virtual figure moves through the stage's overall space. Although its rigid position with widespread arms and the legs pulled together, the body composed of light rays seems to move freely: elevating itself in front of Barthès, it flies over the dancer's head in order to dive to the floor afterwards. In the following moments, the blue-coloured figure demonstrates a performance which transcends man's physical capacities. For example, the virtual dancer does not only move without animating its feet but it also effectuates numerous turns with widespread legs, accelerating the movement up to superhuman speed. More than this, the virtual body's jumps apparently obey a different, weaker gravity as it falls much slower than a human body would. Furthermore, in certain moments the figure's movement on stage is so quick that it can hardly be followed by human eyes. The virtual dancer's difference is also underlined by the fact

---

[98]"... Drehungen und Hebungen, die ein im Tanz schon immer benutztes Mittel zur Überwindung der Schwerkraft darstellen"
[99] In this context, it is notable to mention that although projected on a two-dimensional surface, the three-dimensional projections have an almost tangible effect.

that although both performers share the same body posture, Barthès is bound to one and the same spot on stage while the figure consisting of blue light occupies diverse places in space and demonstrates a multiple repertoire of anatomically impossible movements.

During its entering on stage, the wire-framed body manifests its virtual nature, demonstrating a different spatiality as well as a non-organic existence, its materiality being reduced to a bundle of light rays projected on a layer of tulle. Also the virtual figure's motion-characteristics differ from those of Barthès. Here, the co-presence of a human dancer and the synthetic figure reveals that their respective bodies belong to different realities; their superposition as well as the resulting relation between both dancers create a tension and even lead to the impression that the virtual body's capacities are superior to Barthès' performance. The two dancers' realities seem to offend each other rather than being compatible.

This impression changes when the synthetic dancer positions himself in front of his human partner and both bodies start to dance simultaneously. The juxtaposition of both bodies reveals that the blue projection possesses Barthès' exact morphology. During this virtual *pas de deux*, the dancer and his synthetic counterpart perform the same steps in complete synchrony as their movements are of the same complexity and obey to the same anatomical rules. Here, the virtual body loses its rigidity in rotating its arms like Barthès in order to fall to the ground and move around its axis afterwards. Although they considerably approach each other, the performances of both bodies differ in their fluidity: despite its plastic aspect and its shimmering surface, making allusion to the slight somatic vibration inherent to every human being, the virtual body's movement is more abrupt and appears less attracted by gravity. Barthès' performance has changed, too, as the dancer now seems to concentrate less on his own body but also watches the virtual appearance, attentive for synchronic movement.

If in the piece's beginning, Barthès as well as the wire-framed figure demonstrated and expressed their particularities through distinct ways of moving, it is also their dance which allows both bodies to approach each other in this passage. Here, especially the virtual figure seems to adopt human-like characteristics, as it leaves its freedom in space in order to perform on the stage floor, together with Barthès. However, several of its virtual characteristics remain in the synthetic body's movement.

While the two dancers previously approached each other through their movements, they even enter into 'physical contact' in the following sequence, as the virtual body stretches out its hand and 'touches' Barthès. Now, both performers enter into a dialogue, as the virtual figure is being stretched to the ground and lifted up by Barthès. Moreover, the choreographer even performs artistic exercises in lifting his synthetic counterpart above his head. During this performance, his 'partner' demonstrates a human-like physicalness as 'he' seems to have weight and thus resembles a 'real' dancer subject to gravity.

The physical contact (if one might designate it as such) between the dancer and his virtual partner consists in the projection of the virtual figure's light rays onto a part of Barthès' body. Although these moments are but another demonstration of both performers' difference, it is precisely here that corporeal and virtual reality seem to meet, to communicate. Through their interaction, the two dancers become partners; in these moments, their performance is melted as both bodies rely on each other.

In the choreography's end, Barthès finds himself alone on stage; he performs a solo sequence. This time, the style of his movement has changed, as its transitions are more abrupt and the entire sequence of steps appears more fragmented. This contrasts with the dancer's fluid performance in the piece's beginning. When the virtualised sounds intensify and create a quick rhythmic beat, Barthès' body starts shaking and expressively moves his head and arms. The shaking's intensity gradually increases; it grows in strength and aggressiveness until the dancer ends up with his body inflected forwards, waving his arms without interruption. By now, the music has transformed into a mechanic, aggressive sound which underlines the character of Barthès' actual performance. At this moment, the virtual dancer reappears on stage; it approaches Barthès from behind in the same position, bent-over and equally heavily shaking. But the wire-framed body does not stay alone, as more of its species are projected on the tulle screen which now form a group of seven virtual actors in different sizes, all performing the same shaking movement. Every one of the 'light bodies' unstoppably draws nearer to Barthès who does not advance at all. The stage now presents a monotonous, almost primitive tableau created by each body's simple and rhythmic movement. Suddenly, in the moment before the first virtual body reaches the human dancer, the group of wire-framed figures melts into one light spot which abruptly disappears into Barthès' body. In the next second, the choreographer himself disappears from sight as the stage light is switched off: *Double Cue* is finished.

Although in the choreography's end, Barthès seems to resist the synthetic characters' influence as it is the latter which are vanishing in his organic corpus, *Double Cue* demonstrates the evolving approach between a human body and a virtual, technologically animated figure. The emerging relation between the two bodies goes as far as the synthetic body is even achieving the status of an actor: it becomes Barthès' partner. This fact makes clear that the artificial dancer's role transcends the task of pure representation, as it possesses a proper materiality as well as distinct characteristics. As *Double Cue* shows, both bodies seem equated in the moment of performance. How has this equality been achieved, and how precisely did both dancers overcome their differences?

3.3 Performing with *Poser*: dialogue and exchange

Double Cue shows that in order to perform together, the choreography's interpreters open themselves to each other; this means that every dancer responds to the proper characteristics of his respective partner. In Barthès' creation, the virtual body adopts human characteristics while the organic dancer's movements gradually change into more abrupt, mechanical steps. Thus, the mutual influence of the two dancers is rendered on stage; the superposition of virtual and live body in the same performance space produces both new visual experiences as well as new meanings.

Nevertheless, one has to be conscious of the fact that the piece's performance is entirely prescribed as it has been rehearsed beforehand. Thus, also the preparations and repetitions for *Double Cue*'s performance witness a strong interplay between human and technological capacities and show that in the piece's creation, digital and human work are intertwined. In order to analyse *Poser*'s influence on Barthès' performance as well as on the creative process in this section, I consider it necessary to give a summary of the software's functioning.

3.3.1 The software *Poser*

Poser is a computer program designed for the creation and animation of virtual, three-dimensional figures. It is used in various domains for the simulation of human, animal or machine movement. Since its creation in 1996[100], the software has known different versions aiming at a most realistic animation of virtual characters. It is notable that the efficient application of *Poser* demands a high level of computer literacy and practice and is thus mostly reserved to specialists such as multimedia experts and artists. *Double Cue* too results from a collaboration between Patrice Barthès and a multimedia artist, Fabrice Nourrichard. As the virtual characters' creation and animation with *Poser* does not require any direct contact with a physically existing body, it seems to move one step further in the direction of disembodiment:

---

[100] retrieved June 2nd, 2006, from http://www.e-frontier.com/go/poser_hpl.

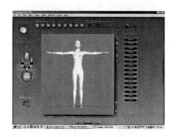

Figs. 3.1,3.2,3.3 (top to bottom):
different designs of characters created with
Poser

the synthetic figures as well as their actions seem to be exclusively based on algorithmic calculation.

The creation of a virtual character with *Poser* is based on the modulation of a prototype already proposed by the software program. This means that the user can choose between different categories of three-dimensional bodies[101] which are displayed on the computer screen. The chosen model then serves as 'raw material' for the desired figure as it can be manually modified: a wide range of aspects such as details in the body form and body parts but also facial expressions can be adapted to the user's ideas. The software's menu allows the figure's modulation via data input (for example, the size of a body part can be indicated in numbers) or the direct manipulation with the cursor[102]. Fabrice Nourrichard explains that as the virtual dancer in the case of *Double Cue* possesses Barthès' morphology, the man's physical shape had to be translated onto the digital body. Therefore, the multimedia artist "took photographs from Patrice [Barthès] standing in a fixed position on stage. The photographs … were taken from different angles. Then I transmitted [the dancer's] dimensions onto the *Poser* model in forming it with the cursor"[103]. Once a digital model is 'personalised', it "can be rendered as wireframe, skeleton, silhouette or figure", as announces the software company *e-frontier* which develops and distributes all versions of *Poser*[104]. Thus, the created figure's form can vary from a very realistic to a more conceptual appearance, like in the

---

[101] The different categories are based on various body forms. Thus, not only the choice between the figure's sex is given but also its age, size etc. (retrieved June 2nd, 2006, from http://www.e-frontier.com/go/poser_hpl).
[102] For example, longer ears can be achieved in simply pulling them with the computer mouse's cursor (retrieved June 2nd, 2006, from http://www.e-frontier.com/go/poser6/features).
[103] Fabrice Nourrichard's quotations are resulting from a telephonic interview held on June 2nd, 2006.
[104] (retrieved June 2nd, 2006, from http://www.e-frontier.com/go/poser6/features).

example of *Double Cue* (figs. 3.1-3.3). The manifold possibilities proposed by this software illustrate Günter Berghaus' description of virtuality as a possible form and respectively as several concepts of reality (chapter 2.3.1), as one model can exist in various formats. Thus, each modelled character is but one choice amidst a wide range of potential realities.

The creation of each *Poser* character is effectuated via computer programming and thus not through the direct contact with a 'real' body model; hence it relies on a digital prototype. This prototype however is based on true human forms whose proportions and dimensions have been digitised and consequently entered the software's data-driven system[105]. Thus, we see that the figure which seems to be an entirely computational product nevertheless relies on a human base. Furthermore, these models are modulated by a programmer; another time the software is not free from human intervention.

This aspect becomes equally clear in the animation of a *Poser* figure which is based on the principle of interpolation. Here, the user's involvement may at first sight appear as limited because the virtual movement itself is indeed generated by the software and human intervention merely consists in the indication of the movement's start and ending. For instance, in order to animate the left arm of a figure, the user indicates a first position from which the movement is supposed to start (figure A) and a second position in which the animation should end (figure B). Once this information is transmitted to the computer, *Poser* is able to interpret the movement between both positions with the help of algorithmic calculation[106]. The body's movement is then displayed on the *Poser* menu in the form of a timeline (see for example the timeline of face movement in fig. 3.4). Like in the process of Motion Capturing (chapter 2.3.2), *Poser* understands movement as the relation of defined points to each other. Nevertheless, *Poser* distinguishes itself through the fact that those points are not indicated by a moving human body but are supplied by the software programmer.

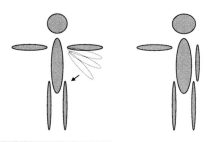

Figures A, B (left to right):
The interpolation process consists of the indication of a start position (A) and an end position (B).
The arm's movement (in the arrow's direction, fig. A) is then interpreted by the software itself.

---

[105] Fabrice Nourrichard.
[106] In figure A, the arm's movement is indicated by the dashed arm positions following the arrow's direction.

At first sight, interpolation might appear as a process which reduces human involvement to a minimum and thus acknowledges a considerable autonomy to the software, as "the computer decides for itself how to maneuver [the virtual figure] from one position [to another]" (De Spain, 2000:5). However, as the movement has to be created for each concerned body part, a complex animation demands the user to consider and work on the various parameters at his disposal. For example, in order to make *Double Cue*'s virtual character dance, Fabrice Nourrichard had to consider parameters comprising the virtual body's hands, forearms, upper arms, shoulders, thorax, pelvis, hip, thighs, trunk, tibia, feet, cervix and head[107]. Here, it is obvious that an articulation between some of those possible body parts requires a complex work of interpolation. This aspect is even reinforced by the fact that in choosing the most direct movement between the figure's starting and end position, *Poser* does not always respect anatomical limits. For instance, a virtual figure supposed to move from one certain point to another will progress in floating on the ground instead of lifting its feet in order to walk, like also *Double Cue*'s character does. Thus, a very detailed indication of interpolation points is

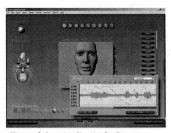

Figure 3.4: a timeline in the Poser menu displays the digital movement's data

necessary. This example does not only demonstrate the particular quality of virtual movement but it also clarifies that animation generated with *Poser* demands a considerable amount of human intervention; the software is thus not an autonomous because it depends on its user's decisions.

Although the digitally created movement is not resulting from any direct contact to a human body, it cannot be considered as purely mechanical, as "the human element is involved in the programming of movement sequences" (Apostolos, 1989:45). *Poser*'s virtual prototypes as well as the interpolation process clarify that at its base, the software relies on human intervention; human work and technology are intertwined in the creation and animation process. Nevertheless, the software's functioning also reveals another interesting point as it makes clear that due to its programmability, each digital character is after all controlled by a *Poser* user. In the case of *Double Cue*, this fact means that although "the computer program becomes an … actor which exists on stage with the dancers …, its autonomy … particularly depends on how man … grants

---

[107] Fabrice Nourrichard.

an independent existence to his virtual partner" [108] (Dinkla, 2000:12). Indeed, as the following sub-sections illustrate, *Double Cue*'s performance and creation have not only been marked by the inter-influence of human and synthetic partners but also by the decision to what extent the virtual movement should be restricted and become adjusted to human properties.

3.3.2 The creation of an *interspace* in digital performance

The integration of digital media and movement creates new virtual and physical realities.

Gretchen Schiller (2002:190)

Like the previously mentioned technologies, also the use of *Poser* inscribes itself into different aspects of dance performance. The software's influence is already reflected in *Double Cue*'s stage design, as contrary to the illuminated stages in conventional dance presentations, the dancers' surrounding in *Double Cue* is characterised by a high level of obscuration. This effect is due to the fact that in order to be visible on the tulle fabric, the virtual figure's projection necessitates a certain degree of darkness. Although the presence of a screen on stage has already been introduced in the context of video performance (chapter 2.2), the space presented through video projection is limited to two dimensions. Also the projection surface in *Double Cue*'s performance is two-dimensional as it merely consists of one tulle layer. Nevertheless, as the fabric is transparent, the stage's space behind it is still visible. This fact allows a certain depth to the projection, granting it more plasticity and a three-dimensional optic when watched from the audience's perspective[109].

The tulle's transparency has a supplementary effect, as with its help, Patrice Barthès juxtaposes and thus confronts the theatrical stage with *Poser*'s synthetic space. Here, Virtual Reality finds itself introduced to the 'real' dance stage; in this concrete comparison, VR's immaterial character becomes especially clear. This idea is even reinforced through the three-dimensional appearance of the computed dancer, as he now moves not only in virtual spheres, but also in a materially existing space; this arrangement produces the impression of that which Kerstin Evert designs as a "theatre-on-the-theatre" (Evert, 2003:101). Not only is the projection's artificial nature

---

[108] "Das Computerprogramm wird zum ... Akteur, der auf der Bühne eine Existenz mit den Tänzern... führt. Seine Autonomie... hängt vor allem davon ab, inwieweit der Mensch... seinem virtuellen Partner ein Eigenleben zugesteht."
[109] In this context, the British media artist Paul Sermon advances the question if the three-dimensional effect of projections on fabric screens is not but an effect to the spectator's media-accustomed eye (Leeker, 2002).

underlined here, this juxtaposition also makes allusion to the representational character of the stage itself: notwithstanding its material existence, the stage's aim is the representation and simulation of characters and events[110]. In her work *Computers as Theatre*, Brenda Laurel explains that in theatre, we understand " 'reality' [as that] what happens in an imaginary world on the stage - [which is simply] a representation" (Laurel, 1993:16). Thus, visible parallels are drawn between VR and the theatrical podium. In this context, Evert states that "the screen as a second stage [creates] an analogy between Virtual Reality as simulation technology and theatre as illusionary space" (2003:101).

Regarding the fact that the computer-generated body is created by algorithmic calculation and given form by several rays of blue light projected on a layer of fabric, its space is intangible, exclusively materialised by the tulle's surface. As it is this layer of fabric which allows the virtual space to enter the materially existing stage, the tulle adopts the function of an interface which resembles a 'transparent screen'. Nevertheless, in *Double Cue*'s beginning these two different spaces rather seem to co-exist as they appear irreconcilable through the dancers' very different performances. It is in the moments of the two bodies' interaction that Barthès and his wire-framed double create a sort of third reality which I want to call an *interspace*. Here, the space 'in between' adopts a mediating function in allowing a (temporary) fusion of virtual space and physical reality. In this context, the choreographer Gretchen Schiller states that the "dynamic and interaction between spaces collectively fall into a new conceptual ... space" (Schiller, 2002:190). Thanks to the *interspace*, both universes seem to be permeable for each other, as they are caught in a dialogue. As will be described in more detail in the following sub-section (3.3.3), the virtual dancer adopts human-like characteristics in order to perform with its organic partner, but also Barthès' performance is highly affected by his wire-framed counterpart. Thus, the virtual figure appears to partly step out of its synthetic realm while Barthès opens himself to computational reality; the *interspace* can consequently be understood as a "space of reciprocal transformation" (Portanova, 2005) in which both parts negotiate their common existence. Here, it becomes clear that, as the Italian researcher Stamatia Portanova explains, "the interface is only a node in the circle" (2005) as also the bodies' interaction and the dynamism between their spaces contribute to the fact that "human and machine ... are in transformational co-adaptation to one another, in a space of non-exclusion" (Massumi, 1995). As in the *interspace*, "all bodies become ... connected" (Portanova, 2005), it does not give way to any domination but rather allows that

---

[110] One example for this is the symbolical character of the stage decorum, where photographs or paintings of houses are sensed to represent real buildings, or the artificial because practiced performance of theatre actors.

human and technological qualities participate in the same process (2005). Here the relation between organic and synthetic space reveals as symbiotic; Barthès and his virtual partner appear to meet in a seamless space which transcends and thus dissolves their (im)material differences.

Furthermore, the *interspace* affects the temporal aspect of each performance as its creation happens in the 'here and now' of *Double Cue*'s presentation. It is thus inseparable from the particular time and place of its becoming and in consequence underlines each representation's live character.

Needless to say, Evert's recently mentioned concept of the "theatre-on-the-theatre" is applicable on the two actors in *Double Cue*, as here the digital and programmed *Poser* figure is confronted with an organic dancer. As already mentioned, a dancer's body is learned, mechanised and thus also 'programmed' in a certain way, and each *Poser* character relies on human intervention. Consequently, both dancers are not confronted with each other in complete dichotomy. Following the idea of the *interspace*, their concerted performance rather creates a sort of common language which particularly affected both dancers during the creative and rehearsal procedure.

3.3.3 *Poser*'s influence on the creative process

> *An important part of this work was the appropriation of the [virtual] double's language. After this process, I didn't dance like before.*
>
> Patrice Barthès

On stage, the mutual influence of the virtual and the organic body is particularly visible in the wire-framed dancer's presentation. Its immaterial, malleable form is especially manifested in *Double Cue*'s beginning, as the virtual body is moulded by several lines forming a "geometric landscape"[111] before they take a human shape: although the synthetic dancer adopts Barthès' morphology, its base is not bound to any organic material. But also its distinct manner of taking the stage's space clearly shows that the projected dancer exists in a different reality. Therefore, the virtual performer adapts himself to Barthès' nature in order to perform a *pas de deux* with the human dancer. For instance, 'he' descends onto the floor and takes the stage's space like his organic partner does. Furthermore, the wire-framed figure abandons its rigidity and adopts

---

[111] Fabrice Nourrichard.

physical characteristics such as slight oscillations and the expression of density and weight; indeed, as Barthès puts it, "[the projected actor] takes an amazingly human character". However, one has to remember that the wire-framed dancer's performance does not happen spontaneously as its movements have been programmed beforehand.

While the virtual figure's adaptation to its human counterpart is very present in the choreography, Barthès' adjustment to his partner's properties is effectuated in a more invisible manner. Nevertheless, also the dancer approaches the synthetic body in translating virtual characteristics into his movement. "In fact, my performance is marked by a permanent dialogue between this synthetic body and myself", explains Barthès. For instance, Barthès' dance is exclusively effectuated in proximity to the transparent screen, thus at the stage's front part. Compared to conventional stage presentations, space is used differently here as the stage's depth is only rudimentarily exploited. However, the synthetic dancer's influence manifests itself also directly in Barthès' bodily performance as the dancer's movement has been formed during *Double Cue*'s creation. For example, during the creative process certain steps were originally choreographed for the virtual figure and subsequently learned by the dancer-choreographer himself. Consequently, the dancer's body had to incorporate movements created for a non-organic corpus. In certain situations, this fact leads to difficulties which can only hardly be overcome. For instance, Barthès explains that in the *pas de deux*' beginning, both dancers move their arms in the air during almost four minutes. While this exercise does not cause any problems to an artificial body, the human performer encounters difficulties as he experiences "an enormous amount of craft and pain"[112] during this presentation. Nevertheless, Barthès' statement "I do it because [the *Poser* model] dances this way. Otherwise, I would never dance like this" shows that his performance is resulting from the software's influence. In this context, another example illustrates Barthès' intensive dialogue with the virtual figure's (im)materiality. In *Double Cue*'s step arrangement, the choreographer introduces a *croisé en arrière-gauche*, i.e. a movement in which the left foot crosses behind the right heel. However, like already mentioned, in the process of animation *Poser* uses the shortest distance between the two interpolation points. This means that when programmed, the virtual figure does not cross its foot *behind* the right leg but goes directly *through* it as it is not bound to anatomical limits. "Here, the question appeared whether the software should be constrained in order to gain a more human character, or if part of its properties should be preserved", mentions Barthès, "and in this particular case, I decided to adapt myself to my virtual partner's performance". Thus, the dancer imitates the artificially created

---

[112] Patrice Barthès.

movement as far as anatomically possible: instead of moving his foot behind his right leg, he crosses the left foot under his lifted right heel. Although this change might appear minimal, it gains importance in the context of dance performance because here, like explained in chapter 1, every step is defined into the smallest detail. This example shows that also the software's properties influence and inscribe themselves into Barthès' choreographic presentation.

In this context, it is worth mentioning that the work with a projection also affects Barthès' spatial orientation. Although the virtual dancer has a three-dimensional effect for the audience, at its base the projection's space is two-dimensional because it is limited to the screen's dimension. Thus, as Barthès is performing close to the screen, he experiences his virtual partner as two-dimensional[113]. This fact implies that the dancer-choreographer has to orient himself not only in the stage's space but also in relation to a 'moving picture' without plasticity nor substance. Here, the artist's only orientation points are provided by the movement happening on screen and thus become more abstract than a human partner's body. Barthès underlines that "it took [him] a considerable amount of time to learn to orientate [himself] in the constellation combining the stage, [his own] body and the interface".

If the work with *Poser* influenced dance performance on different levels, it also affected and transformed the choreographic process, as a third actor became involved for *Double Cue*'s composition. Every dance production integrates the work of two parts, namely the choreographer deciding about the movement sequences which are to be presented, and the performers of those steps, thus the dancers. It is already in this context that *Double Cue* is a particular case, as here, the work's creator and performer are one and the same person. Nevertheless, as the integration of a software program requires specific computer knowledge and skills, Barthès had to collaborate with the multimedia artist Fabrice Nourrichard. As a consequence, a supplementary part was introduced in the choreographic process in order to create and animate *Double Cue*'s virtual dancer. This means that Barthès' ideas concerning the digital body's movement had to be transmitted to Fabrice Nourrichard who himself programmed the computer-generated animation. The new constellation had several consequences on the creative process as it was marked by a close exchange between the two artists.

Being a multimedia specialist, Fabrice Nourrichard is not particularly familiar with dance performance. Thus, he first had to learn to understand Barthès' choreographic ideas before translating them into digital movement. To find out which body parts are the most concerned in certain dance sequences, Nourrichard not only followed Barthès' movements intensively but he

---

[113] ibid.

also "listened to [his] own body" in imitating the prescribed steps himself. This way, he detected the appropriate interpolation points for the movement's numerical writing[114]. Here, it becomes visible that the performance of *Double Cue*'s digital dancer not only integrates the choreographer's ideas but also Nourrichard's understanding and experience of the effectuated movement.

During the piece's creation, also the dancer-choreographer had to gain a certain knowledge of Nourrichard's work with *Poser*. Being informed about the software's properties and functioning, Barthès was able to understand the difficulties of the interpolation process and the involved need of time. According to the choreographer, "it was only when [he] knew how *Poser* worked that [he] understood that the digital creation of a complex movement takes a considerable amount of time. ... When there were many interpolation points to coordinate, Fabrice [Nourrichard] would spend one week in order to make the digital dancer perform for one minute". It is also due to these circumstances that in certain situations, Nourrichard and Barthès decided to leave some liberty to the software's interpretation, as the interpolation process would have required a too important temporal investment[115]. In those situations, Barthès adapted himself to the virtual dancer's characteristics, as illustrate the examples presented earlier in this section. Here, it becomes clear that the creative process is not linear any more, understanding the choreographer as the source of ideas and the performer as their mere receiver, as also the digital dancer's characteristics inspire Barthès as creator. Here, the learning process loses its unilateral direction, giving way to a rather "choreo-technical relation" (Portanova, 2005) between the involved parts.

In an overall view on his work with *Poser*, Patrice Barthès explains that he "unlearned [his] dance" in adapting his performance to the virtual partner's characteristics; according to the artist, this process made him abandon his usual moving and orientation patterns. In this context, also Portanova explains that a consequence of the contact between human body and technology is the fact that "the human body stumbles and slips into unknown and disorienting patterns" (2005). In the case of *Double Cue*, Portanova's thought is illustrated amongst others through the introduction of new structures in Barthès' spatial orientation as well as in the piece's creative process. Nevertheless, this idea does not have to be understood as making the dancer become lost in an insurmountable situation, as the example of *Double Cue* shows that Barthès is not *un*learning his dance but he rather *re*learns it. Although Barthès may qualify parts of his

---

[114] Fabrice Nourrichard.
[115] In this context, Barthès explains that the creation of *Double Cue* required the amount of 1000 working hours, contrary to 500 hours for conventional productions.

previously acquired technique as inappropriate in the perspective of multimedia performance, he gradually learned to adapt to the used technology. During this process, his dance as well as his body can be considered as being relearned or 'reprogrammed' in a certain way, as Barthès does not lose nor "unlearn" his performance but rather adapts himself in the presence of a new technology. Here, it becomes clear that with the help of *Poser*, "the experimental work on movement allowed to shift mental, learned and anatomical movement boundaries"[116] (Evert, 2003:84). As the dancer integrates characteristics of the software program, the software's use is present and inscribes itself in his body's performance. Moreover, human characteristics and intervention modulate and thus appropriate the technology; the body as well as the software enter into an equal relationship marked by mutual influence. This idea illustrates Soeke Dinkla's statement concerning multimedia application in dance performance: "nowadays, [dance is not concerned with] the progressive overlap of two realities but with the orientation between different layers of reality which are connected to each other, and which are coexisting in an equitable way"[117] (Dinkla, 2000:12-13).

In *Double Cue*'s beginning, it seems that two closed systems, namely *Poser*'s virtual sphere and Barthès' organic reality, coexist. In a Baudrillardian perspective, the *Poser* figure appears very distant from and even dangerous to the human body, as the latter risks to be 'digested' in the process of digitalisation. Nevertheless, the two dancers' gradual approach shows that beyond the definition of computer technologies as an instrument for the simulation of human movement and beyond considerations about the negative and decomposing character of New Technologies, "technology appears as a way to discover new ... possibilities still unexplored in the limited frame of the human body" (Portanova, 2005). It is precisely in the *interspace*, the intersection between both bodies that organic and virtual qualities become exchanged and human corpus and software program negotiate a new relationship which affects different processes in the field of dance performance. Once again, like in the example of the pointe shoe or video performance, dance has appropriated part of the used technology. Thus, through constant exchange and openness to one another, technology and human body establish a very close relationship. Their tight connection even reaches the point that in certain moments, both components are not distinguishable anymore. This level is for example achieved when Barthès and his virtual partner negotiate their *pas de deux*, as the resulting movements cannot be clearly attributed to the

---

[116] "... die Arbeit am Bewegungsexperiment erlaubte, mentale, erlernte und anatomische Bewegungsbegrenzungen zu verschieben"
[117] "heute [geht es im Tanz] nicht mehr nur um eine fortschreitende Überlagerung zweier Realitäten, sondern um die Orientierung in miteinander vernetzten Wirklichkeitsebenen..., die gleichberechtigt nebeneinander stehen"

characteristics of one distinct dancer. While the boundaries between the organic and the virtual body's qualities are increasingly blurred, it is also here that their close connection is revealed.

A shift of boundaries is also introduced in *Double Cue*'s creative process. Here, the dance studio transforms into a place of exchange, a *DanceLab*[118] in which new directions and possibilities are explored. The example of *Double Cue* shows that the integration of digital technologies in dance performance not only allows a close exchange between a human dancer and a software's properties but also between two men belonging to different domains. As the virtual dancer also incorporates Nourrichard's experience and reflection on movement, the performance of *Double Cue* allows to integrate a new, an exterior perspective on dance and present it on stage. This fact allows dance to be presented in a self-reflective manner. In the same time, Barthès' creation shows that the work with the digital technology of *Poser* lead both artists to experience, and in Barthès' case even to learn their bodies in a new way.

---

[118] Following the title of Kerstin Evert's work entitled *DanceLab. Zeitgenössischer Tanz und Neue Technologien* (Evert, 2003).

Conclusion

"Beyond the imitation and resemblance of human movement and under a superficial level of realistic representation, a wide range of interesting ... connections are engendered in the relation between the screen, the computer software, and the dancing ... human body", says Portanova when discussing the phenomenon of multimedia performance and analysing the dancer's relation with New Technologies (2005). The researcher's statement clarifies that a perspective on the integration of computer technologies in dance performance should not be limited to the apparent discrepancy between organic body and synthetic technology, as beyond this aspect, both components can be, and already are, linked to each other.

As this thesis has shown, the dancer and technology are in close relation to each other, or in a Maussian perspective, a part of the dancer *is* technology. Furthermore, during the evolution of dance, the performer's corpus adapted itself to the characteristics of various technologies which were integrated into dance performance but which initially were exterior to the human body. The examples of the pointe shoe and video demonstrate how the dancer appropriates the respective instruments in his performance. While the pointe shoe is quasi 'digested' by the human body as it takes an almost prosthetic status, the dancer also appropriates video technology in adapting his movements to the particularities of the camera and of the projection screen. However, the close connection between body and video is rather established by the fact that the recorded images rely on a material base, in this case the human body. As the description of the dancer's engagement with the different devices makes clear, the human-technological relation is also reflected in various aspects of dance performance; here, especially its aesthetics are influenced.

Furthermore, the pointe shoe and video illustrate that their introduction to dance was deeply influenced by socio-cultural circumstances, or as Daniel Sibony puts it, "every dance is bound ... to the culture it derives from"[119] (Sibony, 1995:109). If dance has always experimented with the technologies emerging at different epochs, and if this dance art can be considered as a reflection of society, the integration of NT in dance does not but appear as a logical continuation in the art's development. Consequently, it also seems logical that multimedia performance broaches the much debated issue of disembodiment and the apparent dichotomy reigning between human body and (new) technology. However, the process of Motion Capturing as well as the choreographic work *Double Cue* demonstrate that despite their apparent independence, also New Technologies are relying on a human base. In multimedia performances, the boundaries between

---

[119] "Chaque danse se lie ... à la culture dont elle émane"

human dancer and computer machine become blurred, as for example in the *Mocap* method, the human component is not clearly definable anymore: the technology emancipates physical movement from the organic dancer and subsequently modifies it. This fact nevertheless reveals itself as an extension of the dancer's possibilities rather than restricting him; the performer's engagement with technology allows him to discover new aspects and directions of performance, such as the gain of control over the stage's space, as demonstrates the case of Motion Capturing, or the discovery of new movements and working methods as shown in the example of *Double Cue*.

The presented examples illustrate that the dancer gets into contact with New Technologies through the relearning of his movements and orientation patterns, his 'programming'. In this context, Martina Leeker explains that "as long as man and machine are functioning on the base of programming, they are also able to be connected [to each other]"[120] (Leeker, 2000:15); it is thus through their dance that human performer and technology enter into a dialogue. Following this idea, the example of *Double Cue* even illustrates that in this reciprocal relation, not only the dancer's body is relearned, but technology becomes also anthropomorphised as the piece's virtual dancer adopts human characteristics to perform with his human partner. Here, a symbiotic co-existence is generated because "the machine is made a component of the body and the body a component of the machine" (Berghaus, 2005:224). Although this effect is identified as a threat to corporeality by philosophers such as Baudrillard and Virilio, *Double Cue* has shown that even the virtual dancer's apparent non-referential movement is "ineluctably contexted and referenced through the somatic presence of the performer" (De Spain, 2000:11). The particular role of dance in this context is that it relates the technical animation or simulation of movement to the human body and thus integrates it into a horizon of human experience and comprehension. As a result, multimedia performance is breaking with the myth of New Technologies' disembodying effect as well as the incompatibility of organic bodies and synthetic technologies or figures. Thus, dance as a physical art shows that a symbiotic relation with digital technologies is possible: instead of a suffocated, over-mechanised human body, digital dance (trans)forms the organic body in a "qualitative change" (Portanova, 2005) which gives way to new possibilities and new directions, such as other technologies did before when integrated into artistic performance. Representing a reflection of society, may it even be the task of dance to absorb cultural technologies and point out different ways how to embrace them?

---

[120] "Insofern als Menschen und Maschinen auf der Grundlage von Informationsverarbeitung funktionieren, sind sie auch einander anschlussfähig."

The possibilities originating from a collaboration between dancers and New Media are too important and enriching to be swept away by doubts on the compatibility of organic and computer realities. Like New Technologies' predecessors in their beginnings, also digital technologies are still used in an experimental manner when it comes to dance performances. Nevertheless, it is their application which will allow New Technologies to gradually enter a human context. In an interview with Kent De Spain, the choreographer Merce Cunningham mentioned: "I'm sure that when the typewriter came in everybody said it wasn't human, and then of course you use it and it becomes human" (De Spain, 2002:13).

This thesis has demonstrated that like with 'older' technologies, the dancer's body engages with New Technologies in finding new ways of expression, orientation and performance and thus leaves behind the sharp boundaries between the human body and virtual space. Because "technology is becoming too much a part of every aspect of our lives now ... to be legitimately ignored .... If our dance is to reflect our lives, we must learn to create new movements in new spaces, and dance with the technology within and around us" (De Spain, 2000:16). Digital technologies having an influence on dance's basic elements, notably movement, space and time, their potential to redefine the borders between body and simulation, virtual and material space are quasi inexhaustible. Thus, we cannot but anticipate multimedia performances and their manifold possibilities which are to come in the near future.

References

Apostopolos, Margo (1989).
Programming a Robot to Dance. In: Gray, Judith (ed.) (1989).
Dance Technology: Current Applications and future Trends. Reston Publications

Au, Susan (1988).
Ballet & Modern Dance. London: Thames and Hudson Ltd.

Barringer, J. & Schlesinger, S. (2004).
The Pointe Book. Shoes, training and technique. Hightstown, NJ: Princeton, 2nd edition

Baudrillard, Jean (1994).
Simulacra and Simulations. Ann Arbor: University of Michigan Press (original work published in 1981)

Baudrillard, Jean (1997).
Art and Artefact. London: SAGE

Berghaus, Günter (2005).
Avant-Garde Performance. Live events and electronic technologies. NY: Palgrave Macmillan

Bland, Alexander (1976).
A History of Ballet and Dance. London: London Editions

Cranko, John (1974).
Über den Tanz. Gespräche mit Walter Erich Schäfer. Frankfurt am Main: S. Fischer Verlag

De Leeuwe, H.J. & Uitman, J.E. (1966).
Toneel en Dans. Utrecht: A. Oosthoek's Uitgevermaatschappij

De Spain, Kent (2000).
Dance and Technology: A Pas de Deux for Post-humans. In: *Dance Research Journal,* nr. 32, 2000

De Vroomen, Jacques (2001).
Theater en Techniek. Een historisch overzicht. In: *Theater en Educatie.* Jaargang 7 no.2, 2001: Theater en Nieuwe Media. Verkenningen in Cyberspace.

Dinkla, Sönke (2000).
Vom Zuschauer zum vernetzten Teilnehmer. Über eine neue künstlerische Organisationsform. In *Tanzdrama* nr. 51, 2/2000. Vienna: Theaterverlag Eirich

Dinkla, Sönke & Leeker, Martina (eds., 2002).
Tanz und Technologie. Auf dem Weg zu medialen Inszenierungen. Dance and Technology. Moving towards Media Productions. Berlin: Alexander Verlag

Evert, Kerstin (2003).
DanceLab. Zeitgenössischer Tanz und Neue Technologien. Wurzburg: Königshausen & Neumann

Franklin, Eric (2004).
Conditioning for Dance. Leeds: Human Kinetics

Gray, Judith (ed.) (1989).
Dance Technology: Current Applications and future Trends. Reston Publications

Guest, Ivor (1972).
The Romantic Ballet in England. Its Development, Fulfilment and Decline. London: Pitman Publishing

Kepner, Leslie (1997).
Dance and Digital Media: Troika Ranch and the Art of Technology. In: *Digital Creativity,* Vol.8, April 1997

Kozel, Susan (1994).
Virtual Reality. Choreographing Cyberspace. In: *Dance Theatre Journal.* Vol.11 Spring/Summer 1994

Laurel, Brenda (1993).
Computers as Theatre. Boston: Addison Wesley-Longman

Leeker, Martina (2000).
Tanz ins transhumane Zeitalter. Überlegungen zum Tanz mit Bild- und Informationstechnologie. In: *Tanzdrama* nr. 51, 2/2000. Vienna: Theaterverlag Eirich

Leeker, Martina (2002).
Dance on telematic Stages. An interview with Paul Sermon. In: Dinkla, Sönke & Leeker, Martina (eds., 2002). *Tanz und Technologie. Auf dem Weg zu medialen Inszenierungen. Dance and Technology. Moving towards Media Productions.* Berlin: Alexander Verlag

Manovich, Lev (2001).
The Language of New Media. Massachusetts: The MIT Press

Mauss, Marcel (1992).
Techniques of the Body. In: Crary, J. & Kwinter, S. (Eds.). Incorporations (pp. 454-476). New York: Zone Books (original work published in 1934)

Michael, Mike. (2000). These Boots Are Made for Walking...: Mundane Technology, the Body and Human-Environment Relations. In: *Body & Society,* Vol. 6. London: SAGE Publications

Picon-Vallin, Béatrice (ed.) (1998).
Les Ecrans sur la Scène. Tentations et Résistances de la Scène face aux Images. Lausanne: L'Age d'Homme

Redhead, Steve (2004).
The Paul Virilio Reader. Edinburgh: Edinburgh University Press

Schiller, Gretchen (2002).
Digitally Mediated Movement Spaces. In: Dinkla, Sönke & Leeker, Martina (eds., 2002).
*Tanz und Technologie. Auf dem Weg zu medialen Inszenierungen. Dance and Technology.
Moving towards Media Productions*. Berlin: Alexander Verlag, p. 176-196

Sibony, Daniel (1995).
Le corps et sa danse. Paris: Seuil

Smith-Autard, Jacqueline (2005).
Dance Composition. A practical guide to creative Success in Dance Making. London: A&C
Black, 5th edition

Vaihinger, Dirk (1997).
Virtualität und Realität. Die Fiktionalisierung der Wirklichkeit und die unendliche Information.
In: Krapp, H. & Waegenbaur, T. (Eds.) (1997). *Künstliche Paradiese - Virtuelle Realitäten.
Künstliche Räume in Literatur-, Sozial- und Naturwissenschaften*. Munich: Fink

Vila, Thierry (1998).
Paroles de Corps. La chorégraphie au XXe siècle. Paris: Editions du Chêne

Virilio, Paul (1986).
Ästhetik des Verschwindens. Berlin: Merve (original work published in 1980)

Internet sources

deLahunta, Scott (2000).
Choreographing in Bits and Bytes: Motion Capture, Animation and Software for making Dances.
Retrieved June 3rd, 2006 from http://www.daimi.au.dk/~sdela/bolzano/

Massuni, Brian (1995).
Interface and active Space. Human-Machine Design. Retrieved June 22, 2006 from
http://www.anu.edu.au/HRC/first_and_last/works/interface.htm

Portanova, Stamatia (2005).
The Intensity of Dance: Body, Movement and Sensation across the Screen. In: *Extensions. The
Online Journal for Embodied Technology*. Retrieved April 11, 2006 from
http://www.wac.ucla.edu/extensionsjournal/

Székely, Gábor (1999).
Where are we going? Virtual Reality in Medicine. Retrieved June 10, 2006 from
http://bmj.bmjjournals.com/cgi/content/full/319/7220/1305

Lightning Source UK Ltd.
Milton Keynes UK
UKOW030339020312

188160UK00002B/23/P